In Love with the Whirlwind

When God Takes Your Heart by Storm

Susan Davis
Book Design: Kayla Kimberlin

AuthorHouse™
1663 Liberty Drive
Bloomington, IN 47403
www.authorhouse.com
Phone: 1-800-839-8640

First published by AuthorHouse   04/28/2010

ISBN: 978-1-4490-8856-9 (sc)
ISBN: 978-1-4490-8857-6 (e)

Library of Congress Number: 2010904684

Printed in the United States of America
Bloomington, Indiana

This book is printed on acid-free paper.

In Love with the Whirlwind

When God Takes Your Heart by Storm

Susan Davis
Book Design: Kayla Kimberlin

In Love with the Whirlwind
When God Takes Your Heart by Storm

Exterior design and interior setup: Kayla Kimberlin
BluePawCreations@yahoo.com

Scripture taken from King James
King James Version - Most widely read classic translation of the Bible. Written in 16th Century English, in 1604, King James I of England authorized a new translation of the Bible into English. It was finished in 1611; just 85 years after the first translation of the New Testament into English appeared (Tyndale, 1526). The Authorized Version, or King James Version, quickly became the standard for English-speaking Protestants.

International Standard Book Number: 1-4392-3850-2

Susan Davis
12011 Grebe Circle
Indianapolis, IN 46229
lovethewhirlwind@sbcglobal.net

Introduction

People often wonder if they are willing to step out and be called Christians in front of a world that persecutes and hates Christians, but the fact remains: none of us are even worthy of being called followers of Christ in the first place.

"Dilatasti cor meum"
"Thou hast dilated my heart"

This book was written for the Glory of God—God is good—no one or anything apart from God is good. Think of life apart from God for eternity—never ending eternity—that is we can call eternal hell. This may sound like a lot of "religious speak" to you—but perhaps this will hit home with you in a more direct way—Life apart from God forever will be life eternally without…

…the sound of your child's voice…seeing flowers…the smell of a lovely rose…the comfort of knowing that others care for you…the beauty of sunsets, animals, and stars…love and laughter…tender words of encouragement…a warm lasting hug…friendship…joy everlasting—hell will be devoid of these things—and you will never experience them ever again unless you know Christ as your Savior *and Lord.* This is not my personal truth—this is God's. Moreover, the reason I have written this book is to speak of the good news of Jesus Christ's saving mercy and grace and how it has effected me personally and to implore you to seek God *while He can still be found…*

I debated with myself as to whether to write this book and report the incredible things that happened to me as I pursued friendship with God. I knew that many would deny that these things had happened and I would receive a lot of dissension from those who do not believe what I am reporting. I also came to realize that this book would not be written for those who choose not to believe, but rather for those who the Lord will lead to it and for those whom the Lord plans to reach through it. The Bible is like that too. Not everyone will come to read, value, and cherish the Bible, but so many have and will. So then, I decided to write this book specifically for those who will find comfort and encouragement from it. I am not ashamed to report the experiences you will read about it in this book because of what **Mark 8:34-38** tells me:

Mark 8:34-38: *And when he had called the people unto him with his disciples also, he said unto them, whosoever will come after me, let him deny himself, and take up his cross, and follow me. For whosoever will save his life shall lose it; but whosoever shall lose his life for my sake and the gospel's, the same shall save it. For what shall it profit a man, if he shall gain the whole world, and lose his own soul? Or what shall a man give in exchange for his soul? Whosoever therefore shall be ashamed of me and of my words in this adulterous and sinful generation; of him also shall the Son of man be ashamed, when he cometh in the glory of his Father with the holy angels.*

Point of the Book

Most books make you plow through them so that you can get to the primary point of the book. I am going to tell you up front what the key points are in my book so there is no mystery. This book is about my personal pursuit of God: seeking God and desire for intimacy with God. When you lean in on God, you will soon discover that intimacy with Him leads to supernatural God-given experiences. It is impossible to have an intimate relationship with God and to avoid the supernatural. If you are not experiencing the supernatural, then you may want to ask just how intimate is your relationship with God? This is my prescribed recommendations for seeking and finding God:

-Seek salvation through Jesus Christ. Ask Jesus to save you by believing that He was born to a virgin through God's Holy Spirit, became a divine sinless human, lived and was crucified as a perfect substitute for all of our transgressions and rose again to reign at the right hand of God eternally. And through repenting of all the evil and sins in your life to Him you can be saved (**John 3:16**). Once you believe and accept Christ as your savior, tell someone to confirm your decision and seek other followers of Christ for support. Pray for Jesus to lead you to such people. Do not worry about making yourself a better person before you do this—it is impossible to be the kind of person God wants you to be before you make this decision. So just, *come as you are* **no matter what you have done in your life.**

-Turn (from your former ways—evil and sinfulness) and follow Christ by believing in Him and reading His guidebook for life—the Holy Bible. Ask for guidance from the Holy Spirit to understand the Bible and He will give it to you.

-Find a Bible-believing church (that believes in Jesus as the only Son of God, crucified for our sins) to attend and to be with other church-goers and your new family of God.

-Seek to be baptized in water to publicly declare your love for Christ (and what He did for you) and for the Father, and Holy Spirit.

-Pray every moment you can (praying is simply talking to the Godhead: Jesus Son of God, the Holy Spirit of God, and God the Father) by repenting for sins, praising God, seeking guidance for your life, thanking God, and sharing your thoughts about everything, and by talking to God. You do not need any special ritual to pray—just talk to God, right where you are anytime, anywhere.

-Pray to be baptized and filled by the Holy Spirit and that He would come into your life. Pray for Jesus to be more than just your Savior but, for Him to be your Lord and Master. Surrender your life wholly to Jesus with no reservations—give it all to Him without knowledge of what this might mean that you trust Him fully for your future.

-Continually ask Christ for help in everything—help for understanding His Word when you read it, help for understanding holiness and handling the sin in your life, help for decisions you need to make daily, and help in seeking Him.

-Love God with all your heart, soul, mind, and strength.

-Love your neighbor (everyone else) as yourself.

Seek God in these ways and I promise *you will find Him.* He is not far from any of us and desires for intimacy with His loved ones—namely you.

Here are some more verses about becoming a Christian:

John 1:12: *But as many as received him, to them gave he power to become the sons of God, even to them that believe on his name:*

John 3:16-21: *For God so loved the world, that he gave his only begotten Son, that whosoever believeth in him should not perish, but have everlasting life. For God sent not his Son into the world to condemn the world; but that the world through him might be saved. He that believeth on him is not condemned: but he that believeth not is condemned already, because he hath not believed in the name of the only begotten Son of God. And this is the condemnation, that light is come into the world, and men loved darkness rather than light, because their deeds were evil. For every one that doeth evil hateth the light, neither cometh to the light, lest his deeds should be reproved. But he that doeth truth cometh to the light, that his deeds may be made manifest, that they are wrought in God.*

Romans 3:23: *For all have sinned, and come short of the glory of God.*

Romans 6:23: *For the wages of sin is death; but the gift of God is eternal life through Jesus Christ our Lord.*

Romans 5:6-8: *For when we were yet without strength, in due time Christ died for the ungodly. For scarcely for a righteous man will one die: yet peradventure for a good man some would even dare to die. But God commendeth his love toward us, in that, while we were yet sinners, Christ died for us.*

Romans 10:9-10: *That if thou shalt confess with thy mouth the Lord Jesus, and shalt believe in thine heart that God hath raised him from the dead, thou shalt be saved. For with the heart man believeth unto righteousness; and with the mouth confession is made unto salvation.*

Romans 12:1-2: *I beseech you therefore, brethren, by the mercies of God, that ye present your bodies a living sacrifice, holy, acceptable unto God, which is your reasonable service. And be not conformed to this world: but be ye transformed by the renewing of your mind, that ye may prove what is that good, and acceptable, and perfect, will of God.*

Table of Contents

Chapter One—**Heaven Is a Real Place**…10

Chapter Two—**When God Closes a Door**…14

Chapter Three—**God's Perfect Plan**…17

Chapter Four—**I Am Ruined**…21

Chapter Five—**Ask and Ye Shall Receive**…25

Chapter Six—**I Chose You**…29

Chapter Seven—**Those Amazing Wonders & Signs**…34

Chapter Eight—**Descend from Heaven**…39

Chapter Nine—**Wash Robes**…42

Chapter Ten—**Be Holy**…45

Chapter Eleven—**Spiritual Milestones**…48

Chapter Twelve—**The Whirlwind***…52

Chapter Thirteen—**Electricity**…58

Chapter Fourteen—**God's Message**…61

Chapter Fifteen—**Grains of Sand**…67

Chapter Sixteen—**The Sparrow**…70

Chapter Seventeen—**The Art Museum**…73

Chapter Eighteen—**Gazing on God**…79

Chapter Nineteen—**Song of Solomon**…85

Chapter Twenty—**Commitment to Fullness**…95

Chapter Twenty-one—**Beautiful Words**…102

Chapter Twenty-two—**What I Have Learned**……108

Chapter Twenty-three—**My Grandmother's Final Instruction**…116

Useful Resources…117

Foreword

This is my testimony of the Holy Godhead: Father God, the Lord Jesus Christ, and the Holy Spirit—and it is very personal to me. I was reluctant initially to broadcast my experiences and debated whether I should do it or not—but I believe that God has led me to a decision to do this for *three* primary reasons:

FIRST, if God shines His wonderful light on any of us—who are we to turn and hide that amazing light from others? I believe *His* light is a beautiful gift that *must be* shared.

Luke 8:16: *No man, when he hath lighted a candle, covereth it with a vessel, or putteth it under a bed; but setteth it on a candlestick, that they which enter in may see the light.*

2 Corinthians 4:7: *But we have this treasure in earthen vessels, that the excellency of the power may be of God, and not of us.*

John 20:21: *Then said Jesus to them again, Peace be unto you: as my Father hath sent me, even so send I you.*

Acts 1:8: *But ye shall receive power, after that the Holy Ghost is come upon you: and ye shall be witnesses unto me both in Jerusalem, and in all Judaea, and in Samaria, and unto the uttermost part of the earth.*

Acts 20:24: *But none of these things move me, neither count I my life dear unto myself, so that I might finish my course with joy, and the ministry, which I have received of the Lord Jesus, to testify the gospel of the grace of God.*

Jeremiah 30:2: *Thus speaketh the LORD God of Israel, saying, Write thee all the words that I have spoken unto thee in a book.*

Luke 12:48: *But he that knew not, and did commit things worthy of stripes, shall be beaten with few stripes. For unto whomsoever much is given, of him shall be much required: and to whom men have committed much, of him they will ask the more.*

SECONDLY, I realized that the Lord has both led me to become a communicator by profession and then later He gave me wonderful things to write about and that I must share these experiences. The Lord refers to the wonderful experiences He has given me as "His Testimonies."

Ephesians 2:10: *For we are his workmanship, created in Christ Jesus unto good works, which God hath before ordained that we should walk in them.*

Habakkuk 2:2: *And the LORD answered me, and said, Write the vision, and make it plain upon tables, that he may run that readeth it.*

Galatians 1:20: *Now the things which I write unto you, behold, before God, I lie not.*

1 John 1:5-7: *This then is the message which we have heard of him, and declare unto you, that God is light, and in him is no darkness at all. If we say that we have fellowship with him, and walk in darkness, we lie, and do not the truth: But if we walk in the light, as he is in the light, we have fellowship one with another, and the blood of Jesus Christ his Son cleanseth us from all sin.*

THIRDLY, I wanted to put these things in this written format to reach out to my family and friends who I would never have a chance to sit down with face-to-face to share my personal testimony of Christ and that perhaps they would read this book and also others who I do not even know could read it too. I am but a very fragile earthen vessel used by the Lord—and nothing more.

1 Corinthians 1:27: *But God hath chosen the foolish things of the world to confound the wise; and God hath chosen the weak things of the world to confound the things which are mighty.*

Luke 12:8-9: *Also I say unto you, whosoever shall confess me before men, him shall the Son of man also confess before the angels of God: But he that denieth me before men shall be denied before the angels of God.*

Acts 4:16-21: *Saying, What shall we do to these men? For that indeed a notable miracle hath been done by them is manifest to all them that dwell in Jerusalem; and we cannot deny it. But that it spread no further among the people, let us straitly threaten them, that they speak henceforth to no man in this name. And they called them, and commanded them not to speak at all nor teach in the name of Jesus. But Peter and John answered and said unto them, Whether it be right in the sight of God to hearken unto you more than unto God, judge ye. For we cannot but speak the things which we have seen and heard. So when they had further threatened them, they let them go, finding nothing how they might punish them, because of the people: for all men glorified God for that which was done.*

Deuteronomy 4:9: *Only take heed to thyself, and keep thy soul diligently, lest thou forget the things which thine eyes have seen, and lest they depart from thy heart all the days of thy life: but teach them thy sons, and thy sons' sons*

Psalms 139:16: *Thine eyes did see my substance, yet being imperfect; and in thy book all my members were written, which in continuance were fashioned, when as yet there was none of them.*

Psalms 118:17: *I shall not die, but live, and declare the works of the LORD.*

People say that God does not speak in an audible voice to His children anymore—at least not the way He spoke to His children of the Old Testament. However, what can we say about the meaning of the following verses?

Malachi 3:6: *For I am the LORD, I change not; therefore ye sons of Jacob are not consumed.*

Hebrews 13:8: *Jesus Christ the same yesterday, and today, and forever.*

James 1:17: *Every good gift and every perfect gift is from above, and cometh down from the Father of lights, with whom is no variableness, neither shadow of turning.*

Matthew 13:58: *And he did not many mighty works there because of their unbelief.*

Yes, people change their minds—but Father God, Holy Spirit, and Jesus Son of God—the Godhead—never, ever changes. God not only still speaks audibly to His children, He still works ambitiously in their lives. God says—if you seek me with all your heart—you will find me—I implore you to seek God while you still can.

Daniel 4:2-3: *I thought it good to shew the signs and wonders that the high God hath wrought toward me. How great are his signs! And how mighty are his wonders! His kingdom is an everlasting kingdom, and his dominion is from generation to generation.*

Jeremiah 33:3: *Call unto me and I will answer thee, and show thee great and mighty things, which thou knowest not.*

Daniel 4:2: *It is my pleasure to tell you about the miraculous signs and wonders that the Most High God has performed for me.*

Dedication

God, the Father Who draws us
Jesus Christ, the Son of God Who saves us with His blood
Holy Spirit, the Spirit of God Who sanctifies us with His truth

Chapter One—Heaven Is a Real Place

Heaven Is a Real Place

None other than my own maternal Grandmother, Mary Ann McKinniss, experienced one of the first supernatural experience reports that came my way. My Grandmother, who has since gone on to be with the Lord, was a woman of few words and yet so in love with God. Writing and reciting poetry to the Lord in her later years was how my Grandmother spent her time. She had a near-death experience in which she had heart failure and she was even pronounced clinically dead by the doctors while in the hospital. She came back to life and shared that what she saw was wonderful and she could not use anything from earth to describe what she had seen. She said that she never feared death again after that. This experience left me with a profound curiosity about God and Heaven at an early age, for which I would later try to find answers. When I was about 14-years-old, my Grandmother made it to her incomparable home.

Jesus Leads Me

Jesus led me to Calvary's Cross
Where my sins were counted loss.
Now He leads me o'er paths He trod,
And now, I receive blessings from a loving God.

Jesus leads me, Jesus leads me,
Jesus leads me every day.
Jesus leads me, Jesus leads me
Jesus leads me safely all the way.

He leads me through the dark Gethsemane,
Through times of dreadful agony.
But through His wonderful keeping power
I am brought victorious through this trying hour.

He leads me through the valley
Where sometimes we must be
So as to trust for plenteous grace,
To lift me up to a higher place.

He leads me to the mountain top,
Where flowing blessing never ceases to stop,
Where all His mercies and tender love
Are always coming from above.

He leads me on to eternity,
Where His loving face I then shall see.
And, Oh, the wonders I shall then behold
When I am safe within God's fold.

-Mary Ann McKinniss

When I Pray

When I Pray
All my burdens roll away
And His smiling, beaming face
Seems to brighten up the place.

When I pray
My life, my all at His feet I lay
Then there comes a deep sweet peace
A sudden feeling of relief.

When I pray
All things earthly fade away,
And I feel all secure
With the one so sweet and pure.

When I pray
All my cares are put away,
And I feel content to rest
On my Savior's loving breast.

-Mary Ann McKinniss

Unlocking the Chains of Smoking

When I was a young teenager, I was a regular nag when it came to griping about my Father's long-running love affair with cigarettes. I hated the cigarettes, I hated him smoking them, and I never missed an opportunity to complain to him about them. Hiding them and sneaking matches out of my Dad's reach allowed me to present my personal annoyance with his irritating habit.

Later on in my youthful years, my Father had returned to his Christian roots in a big way and he knew his smoking habit did not line up with his faith. However, this man had been a hard-core addict to smoking with a 25-year career of chain smoking. Quitting was not going to be easy for this dedicated smoker.

One night, my father prayed to God that he wanted him to take away his desire to smoke so that he could quit and he did not care how he did it, even if God had to make him sick to accomplish it (this was truly his request). I am not sure what was on his mind when he made that request (perhaps the Holy Spirit put it in his mind). That very night, my Father came down with a terrible fever, a frightening fever. My Mother explained to me what my Father had asked for and why he was so ill. By the next morning, my Dad's fever had broken and that is not all—this man, who had been a hard-core chain-smoker, had completely quit his nasty hard-to-conquer habit. He even tried to smoke and was no longer interested in smoking. Now this was an early taste for me of the supernatural power of God.

God's Comfort

My next notable experience with God being real and speaking to His children was later when I went to Christian college. During my senior year, a fellow dorm resident, a very sweet young woman, was also someone I had grown to respect as a very reliable person. She was the Daughter of missionary parents. She confided in me that her own Father had died previously and that after the funeral she, her Mother, and Sister had come home following her Dad's burial. As she, her Mother and Sister were all together crying over this sad event, she said that they all heard a voice speak to them, "It's alright, he's with me." This was an incredible revelation to me—that God spoke to His children.

Sadly, after college, I would jump into one job after another in my pursuit of a career in communications—radio and magazines occupied my time for several years out of college. Again, while at one of my jobs, I would meet a fellow employee who shared an extraordinary story about her husband. A fellow co-worker shared a terrific story about her Husband. This man always wanted his Mother to come to Christ. However, his Mother was a nonbeliever, an atheist, and just prior to reaching the end of her life; she had drifted into a coma. Her Son never gave up and read the Bible at her bedside as she laid in a deep coma. Not knowing the condition of her soul, he read to her about the way of salvation through Christ and he held her hand while he read the Bible to her. He asked her if she believed in Christ—and at that one moment she squeezed his hand—that is all she ever did again and remained in a coma until her death. Great as this all is, sadly, I still made everything else my lord and I think that my career took the lead for that position.

On my Mother's lap as a tike is where I made a commitment to Christ. I am sure that I sat on my mother's lap a million times—but I do not remember any other time sitting on her lap, except the moment in time when I made that decision. Funny that is the only time I remember sitting on her lap.

As a child, I was raised an only child because my Brother was 19 years older and he was already leaving home when I was a baby. Church was something that made my Dad very uncomfortable. His Dad, my Grandfather, was very active in church and my Father had grown up going to church all the time, so when my Dad became an adult, church was not on his radar screen.

To find myself, I would play a dangerous game. I flirted with the world enough to look for my identity through friendships and career. While I never really did horrible things (as far as the world would be concerned), I did the worst possible thing. I straddled the fence big time and I really strayed from God. It really makes me sad, when I think how far off the track I managed to get away from God. Only when I really needed Him, did He seem to surface in my mind. We settle into the world that is right in front of us and it takes over our life. Let me just say this—not making a decision either way about God *is a decision*: to not choose God. I would go through my teens, twenties, and most of my thirties making my way through life without God and thinking I had all the answers for myself. The only thing I really had going for myself, through these periods of my life was God's wonderful patience, mercy, grace, and overall tolerance while I was very slowly coming to the end of myself.

God Is *Always* Listening

One snowy afternoon, I was traveling by myself to downtown Indianapolis and this was before everyone had common access to cell phones. While driving on the Interstate and my car decided to quit running right under a dark, cave-like underpass bridge.

As the snow continued to come down, I sat in the dark under this bridge debating on what I might do next. After much self-deliberation, I decided to get out of the car and walk to the nearest exit up the road. As I was walking along the busy downtown Interstate, a young guy in a very old car pulled up and offered to give me a ride. There was a very uneasy feeling I had about this guy and I told him that if he wanted to help me, would he go and call someone to help me—he sped off angrily when I refused to get in the car with him.

Now at this point, I got a little panicky remembering that I was in a scarier section of town. As my panic began to set in—I prayed that God might help me out. Without more than even a minute of time passing by after my prayer—a police officer pulled up and offered to take me to the nearest McDonald's at the next exit where I could call for a ride. Now you could chalk this up to mere coincidence and I could have felt that way, except it happened to me a second time…

God Is *Really* Listening

Perhaps it was only a year later, and I was driving to work one morning by myself on a cold winter day. This time, I was traveling on a kind of remote road and I came up to a big patch of ice in the road. The next thing I know, my car is spinning out of control and my car was thrown into the opposite direction into a ditch on the side of the road.

In my effort to pull myself out of this ditch that I was stuck in, I spun my wheels causing the car just to go deeper into the ditch. Next, I got out of the car and pulled some cardboard out of the trunk hoping to put it under my tires for traction to get out of the hole I seemed to be digging the car ever deeper into. When my attempts to break free looked completely hopeless—once more panic set in as I soon realized I was out in the middle of nowhere and basically defenseless with no means of contacting anyone.

In a final frustrated moment of panic, I immediately cried out for God to help me in my helpless predicament. Within the next minute after my prayer, a young woman driving by alone saw me out in the middle of nowhere and kindly stopped to pick me up. As soon as I got into the car with this young woman, she reached over and turned on a Christian radio station and soon after, she dropped me safely at my office.

Now if I had prayed for help during these two experiences and there had been a lot of time passing between each prayer and rescue—I might have still given God the credit—but to have it happen both times literally immediately after I had prayed for help—makes one sit up and take notice, as I did.

Acts 2:21: *And it shall come to pass, that whosoever shall call on the name of the Lord shall be saved.*

An Angel to the Rescue

As my dear Father's life was winding down—he had become quite ill with a terminally rare blood disorder. He had become quite fragile through this rare sickness. At this time, he was about 79. One time he was coming back from a visit to the doctor with my Mother and they were walking up to their front porch from their car. At this point, Dad still drove himself everywhere since Mom had never really had a driver's license. The weather was cold, wintry, and their front porch was iced over.

It was a weekday and the neighborhood my parents lived in seemed like a ghost town during daytime hours. However, this day on my parent's front porch, after returning home my Dad slipped on the porch ice and started to go down. To my Mother's surprise, a man suddenly seemingly from out of the blue ran up, he caught my Father from behind, and set him back up on his feet. My mother turned around to thank this good Samaritan who had helped them and when she did, she could find him nowhere. He had vanished.

Now the idea that, on a cold winter day, a man could have been walking by and seen another man start to fall down and start to run up to the yard to catch him at just the exact moment he was falling down and then just disappear without being seen again is more than a little impossible. In fact, it would have been virtually impossible for someone strolling by on the sidewalk to discern that my father was at a certain moment about to go down and for that person to decide to make it from the sidewalk to my father's side in time to catch him. That person would have needed to be standing very near and would have to be watching his every move up to that point and suspect that he might possibly take a fall. Truthfully, my Mother who was standing right next to my Father did not even think about my Father falling down there. Had my Dad actually fallen—it would have brought more physical troubles in his severely fragile condition then he already had. My Mother is convinced this was an angel and I am too—no other explanation suffices.

Isaiah 46:4: *And even to your old age I am he; and even to hoar hairs will I carry you: I have made, and I will bear; even I will carry, and will deliver you.*

Chapter Two—When God Closes a Door

When God Closes a Door, He Opens a Window

My Father and I were extremely close. Perhaps it was because I was his only little girl—maybe it was because I was born later in his life and he had more time to appreciate parenting. I know that we were very close and spent many hours together going places and I talked and he listened. Then towards the end of his life, we had a sad year of facing my Dad's rare terminal blood disorder. He was in and out of the hospital a lot his last year and I can remember bringing up White Castle hamburgers for him to eat in the hospital one of those times. I also brought my computer and worked by his bedside so he would not have to be alone there. Mostly he was in and out of the hospital to receive blood platelets because his body could not produce them anymore.

One day, my Mother called for an ambulance and my Dad was transported to the hospital for his last trip on earth. Sadly, he was bleeding to death and in his last hours, he resembled a concentration camp refugee. He knew death was near, so he said his final goodbyes to my Mom—but she just really didn't grasp that this would be her last time to see him in this life.

Now at the hospital, another drama was playing out. My best friend Beverly was a nurse at the same hospital my Father spent a lot of time at during the last year of his life. Oddly, their paths never crossed during that year that my Dad was in and out of the hospital so much…until the day, my Dad died…until God, in His great providence, assigned my best friend to be his nurse.

Now when my Dad arrived to the hospital, Beverly received her next assignment and it was my Dad's file. Immediately she protested to the doctor on staff. She insisted that this was her best friend's Father and she could not take the case. The doctor on staff said that she had no choice but to take the case because there was no one else on staff to take it. Even though none of us was there, he did know who the nurse was who cared for him. God sent Beverly to him in his final hour and he recognized her. Even though I did not arrive at the hospital until it was too late, it was a relief for me to know that my friend was there during a very difficult time for all of us. Beverly and I have been like sisters and our friendship started back when she was in second grade and I was in fourth grade. What a comfort to have my lifelong friend near my Father when I could not be there. God had it all planned out—but that was not all he had planned…

Not more than an hour after I had arrived at the hospital to find my Father had passed away, I had a strange feeling. It was at that point that I believed I might be pregnant. I really did not give it any more thought for a couple weeks because of the sad time following my Father's death and funeral.

Two weeks later and the dust were clearing, but I was just starting to recover from the trauma of dealing with my Father's funeral, grief, and aftermath of it all. One day while I was at work, I caught myself feeling a little dizzy. Soon after I went to my doctor, he gave me a blood test, and sure enough, I learned that I was pregnant. I also discovered that I actually was pregnant the very day my Dad died—the first day that I suspected that I was pregnant. This was literally within an hour of learning my Father had passed away that I should first suspect that I would be having a baby.

Nine months later, my Dad's little Grandson Ethan Edward was born—and amazingly, even though God took someone very special from me, He left me with someone very special too. This was a stunning miracle to me. Truly, this was God closing a door but also opening a window.

Ecclesiastes 3: 1-4:
¹To everything there is a season, and a time to every purpose under the heaven:
²A time to be born, and a time to die; a time to plant, and a time to pluck up that which is planted;
³A time to kill, and a time to heal; a time to break down, and a time to build up;
⁴A time to weep, and a time to laugh; a time to mourn, and a time to dance;

I Understand About the Children

Time passed and I became preoccupied with new motherhood, since Ethan was my first and only child. I knew in the back of my mind that there was a God and I was strongly suspecting at this point that He must love me. After all—it was amazing the way Ethan came at the exact time my Father had passed away. However, no one could have prepared me for what was about to happen to me next.

When Ethan was about three-years-old, I can remember hearing about the Bosnian war going on at the time. It was especially difficult to hear about the little children who had become orphans and wartime refugees who were being led away to camps without their parents. I thought about my own child and it made me sad to think about these children and their situation.

I can remember lying down in bed praying about these poor war-torn Bosnian children. Then, something incredible—inexplicable happened next. I heard a message in my head—I immediately sat up and questioned what had just happened to me—it was unquestionably a direct message from God.

I could note many things about this extraordinary experience:

-The message entered my mind at an incredible rate of speed—we are talking about a brief conversation that arrived in my mind in almost a split second. **It was as if no time had transpired at all.** The only way I can describe it is think of one second in time you know nothing—then the next second you know a lot more then you did the previous second. I cannot explain it in any other way. I knew this message was from God.

-My initial impression was that the person speaking struck me as being both *empathetic* and *authoritative* (both a *lion* and a *lamb*).

Regarding the *authoritative lion* side of Christ:

Matthew 7:29: says about Christ: *For he taught them as one having authority, and not as the scribes.*

Mark 1:27: *And they were all amazed, insomuch that they questioned among themselves, saying, What thing is this? What new doctrine is this? For with authority commandeth he even the unclean spirits, and they do obey him.*

Luke 4:36: *And they were all amazed, and spake among themselves, saying, What a word is this! For with authority and power he commandeth the unclean spirits, and they come out.*

Revelation 5:5: *And one of the elders saith unto me, Weep not: behold, the Lion of the tribe of Judah, the Root of David, hath prevailed to open the book, and to lose the seven seals thereof.*

Regarding the tender *empathetic lamb* side of Christ:

John 1:29: *The next day John seeth Jesus coming unto him, and saith, Behold the Lamb of God, which taketh away the sin of the world.*

1 Peter 1:19: *But with the precious blood of Christ, as of a lamb without blemish and without spot:*

Revelation 5:8: *And when he had taken the book, the four beasts and four and twenty elders fell down before the Lamb, having every one of them harps, and golden vials full of odours, which are the prayers of saints.*

-There was a great sense of urgency about the message.

-The speaker was a "we" with a choir or plural voice (**Isaiah 6:8** says. *Also I heard the voice of the Lord, saying, whom shall I send, and who **will go for us?** Then said I, Here I am; send me.* **Daniel 10:6** *says: His body also was like the beryl, and his face as the appearance of lightning, and his eyes as lamps of fire, and his arms and his feet like in color to polished brass, **and the voice of words like the voice of a multitude.**)*

Here is the message I heard from God:
"I understand about the children, but as many people need to come to Christ as soon as possible because nothing that is going on in this world is as bad as being separated from God for eternity."

I knew that this was not my own thought because, clearly, I had been just praying about children in Bosnia and I was not thinking of anything else. Suddenly, in a brief moment in time, many things happened for me at once:

-I realized that this was a message from God Himself for me.
-I also knew it had to be from God because of the content of the message.
-The message fully explained to me why bad things happen on earth. Because we are all born sinners by the choices made by Adam and Eve in the Garden of Eden at the beginning of time and God is allowing the evil in this world that we are responsible for to continue so that each one of us can have an opportunity to accept Christ and find eternity with God before it's too late.
-I realized many years later that this brief encounter with God had become like the needle of a compass to me—pointing me in the direction I needed to go and to keep my perspective on life in check. I am so thankful for this incredible, life-changing experience.

I have observed that with both Bible characters and modern-day people that once someone has an experience with God, they can never be the same.

After this happened to me I questioned it and of course I wondered—why me? However, I also felt a deep urgency and sense of responsibility to do something—anything at all. Therefore, at church I had been on the communications committee—but communications was merging with evangelism and becoming one committee and it needed a chairperson to head it up. I knew there was a vacancy for this spot—so I decided after hearing from God that perhaps I needed to volunteer to chair the evangelism committee. The next Sunday—I marched into church armed with the idea that I was going to offer to chair the committee. Someone from the nominating committee walked up to me and said that I had been chosen to chair the evangelism committee. Now this seemed so unexplainable to me since I had already decided to volunteer for it. But, I decided that being at that position must be what God wanted me to do.

Cancer—the Ugly "C" Word
A couple years later, I had gone for my annual mammogram only to be called back in because the test had looked suspicious. After a long wait, I went back for a second mammogram and an ultra-sound. At this point, I was getting nervous and then I am told I need a biopsy. However, this is before Christmas and they cannot get me in for the test until after the holidays. This becomes a very difficult holiday. The day of the biopsy is nerve racking but the technician assures me that it looks like nothing.

Prior to this happening, I wanted to quit my position of evangelism chair at church. It had become frustrating to me and I felt that I was not accomplishing what I needed to and perhaps someone else could do better. A couple of my close friends on the committee called me and asked me to stay on as chair—but I was not convinced that this was where I belonged.

During the biopsy and through the final stages of the testing I pleaded my case to God. I promised that even though I was quite burned out, I would go back and do evangelism at the church—if only He would save me from the possibility of cancer. Now I do not know if God always works like this—but in my case I was given a clean bill of health after a series of scares. I walked away knowing I had to go back to evangelism and try again. I had promised.

Chapter Three—God's Perfect Plan

God's Perfect Plan
Jeremiah 29:11: For I know the thoughts that I think toward you, saith the LORD, thoughts of peace, and not of evil, to give you an expected end.

I have never been more encouraged than after I heard the section Rick Warren wrote about in his highly popular *"40 Days of Purpose"* book that God wanted a friendship with me. When I heard Rick Warren describe this, I was "wowed" and touched that God would want such a personal relationship with me. If God wants such a relationship with me, I thought, than who am I to keep that from happening? Thus began my pursuit of the lover of my soul and I was not ready for what was to happen next.

Now one of my prayers that I prayed frequently to God was that since He had created me, I was sure that He had a perfect plan for my life. If I gave Him my life then He could apply His perfect plan to my life. I was tired of trying to run my own life and I was sure what He had planned was much better than any plans I could come up with. I know the things that happened after this point most probably had to do with completely surrendering my life to God and my new desire to seek to know God specifically as a friend. I reminded Him frequently that I was interested in being His friend and having His friendship would mean so much to me.

God communicated to me in some awesome ways and I am sure there will be those who doubt these highly coincidental episodes as questionable—but to me they were precious moments.

Heaven Researched
It all started with a book my brother gave me about Heaven. I read a book written all about Heaven and I even listened to the CD in my car about the same book. Whenever I get it in my head to find out about a topic of any kind—I usually become obsessive about it. Other past obsessions have been my career and books revolving around that, but this topic "Heaven" really had me intrigued so I brought home many books from the library about this subject.

One such book was about a woman's visions of Heaven. In it she says that Jesus told her we give, our worldly interests more time than we give Him—I realized this was very true about me. One cannot research Heaven without learning about the reality of hell, and the requirements of access to Heaven. This is written plainly in the Bible. I began to take inventory of my life and I knew that my life did not meet up to the standards of the Bible. God just did not receive much of my time.

Mark 12:30: *And thou shalt love the Lord thy God with all thy heart, and with all thy soul, and with all thy mind, and with all thy strength: this is the first commandment.*

Jesus considered this commandment the first most important commandment of the ten. Well, what is the opposite of the commandment love the Lord your God with all your soul, heart, mind, and strength? Would it be, not loving the Lord your God with all your soul, heart, mind, and strength? If you do not spend much time with the Lord, then you can hardly say that you observe this commandment.

My focus had not been on God, but rather my career and all sorts of other things. Changes needed to be made in my life to bring more of God into it. But, just exactly how could I do this I wondered? My life was already full of so much busyness: domestic work, my son, caring for an elderly parent, and even church activities kept me busy. In addition, I had taken on a very big marketing project which was my intense focus at that time and it drained away my time.

I so wanted to give God more of my time—but how? Strategic planning and some thought would have to go into this process. Since I worked from home, I often watched TV while I ate lunch. Off the TV went at lunch (nothing I watched was good anyway). In its place, I opened up the Bible and started a regimen of reading daily. Starting with the New Testament, I read it several times during my lunch hour. I knew that God was omniscient and omnipotent—also that He heard our prayers all the time. What better opportunity to talk to God I thought right in my car with all the running around that I did alone. Therefore, I set out to talk to God every chance I could when I was alone in my "chapel" car—and I still *love* to talk to God whenever I am alone.

In the meantime, I received criticism from those around me for reading and believing books written by people who had visions of heaven. This greatly saddened me since I found that these profound experiences made me take great inventory of my life in relation to God. My commitment to God was bankrupt despite my proclamation that I was a Christian and all my Sunday morning church routines and involvement. These books talking about other people's visions of Heaven was the wakeup call I needed…but how could this information be false I wondered? I needed to find out for myself somehow.

Now research has been my thing. When I wanted information about a subject matter—I could be fanatical about it. If I really liked a certain subject, I could go crazy digging up all the latest details surrounding it. I applied this same heated obsession to finding out about Heaven. Book after book later, about people who had both Heaven visions and near-death experiences, I devoured. Then I discovered a remarkable thing. I began to notice that what these people all had in common were minuscule details that they could not have all noted—unless they had actually seen the same things. When I noticed this, I started to put together a research paper cataloging my findings. These details were so extremely minor, yet significant, that had these people not shared these experiences and reported what they had seen then there is no possible way they would have known to report these very tiny details of what they had seen.

The best way to describe this phenomenon would be to ask five people to describe to me their trips to China. Let us say I myself had never been to China and I wanted to know all about it and these five people describe to me their personal experiences. Because of China's vastness, all five share very different stories, however each one describes one tiny detail, which there is no way they would combined know unless they in fact had been there and indeed were telling the truth! This would then tell me that their stories all were most likely true and believable as well. This is what I discovered in my research of the stories people told of their visions and near-death experiences of Heaven. The findings were remarkable. I could not believe what I was stumbling onto. However, I now believe that God wanted me to discover these truths—because I was seeking God with all my heart. *The incredible findings that I turned up are free upon request by contacting me through email. My "Heaven Researched Report can be obtained by emailing lovethewhirlwind@sbcglobal.net and simply requesting a copy.*

1 Corinthians 2:9-10: *But as it is written, Eye hath not seen, nor ear heard, neither have entered into the heart of man, the things which God hath prepared for them that love him. But God hath revealed them unto us by his Spirit: for the Spirit searcheth all things, yea, the deep things of God.*

Fear Life or the Lord
While going through this process of seeking God I was simultaneously struggling with incredible personal fears. I had people who depended on me—my son and my mother—but also my best friend was going through difficult times and I just felt great fear that something might happen to me. I feared greatly whenever I needed to drive across town—what would happen to those who needed me if something happened to me? Now I know this sounds ridiculous to some people—but to me it was a very real problematic fear.

This fear had escalated to the point that I could almost not function anymore. One day while I was alone in the house and I spoke to God regarding my fears and how they seemed to incapacitate me. Admittedly, they were controlling me. Down on my knees before Him I admitted that I no longer wanted control of my life. I wanted to give Him my fears and control. In fact, I heartily begged Him to take these fears from me. Then incredibly these fears, that controlled me, were absolutely taken from me. I have no way to explain it, but I felt I was really giving them to God and I felt He had really taken them from me. And He had. It was a beautiful thing.

Psalms 34:4: *I sought the LORD, and he heard me, and delivered me from all my fears.*

Now I had previously mentioned my desire to find ways to spend more time with God and often I would talk with Him in my car. I found myself talking with Him frequently as if He were right there in the car with me and I considered Him to be a wonderful friend who would listen without response. This was even reminiscent of days spent with my own earthly Father who was a great listener and would listen to me carrying on about the latest tale I had to tell. For a while, this seemed like such a one-sided friendship between God and me—but really I did not expect anything else—ever. I never imagined in my wildest dreams that I would ever really actually hear anything from God. I really did want to believe that He was listening to me carrying on with Him conversations about my day and what was currently on my mind. Crazily I often would say things to Him like, "I know you are listening." I really knew He was listening—but I was completely unprepared for the idea that God would actually return my calls (so to speak). It was comforting just knowing that most likely *He was* listening to me and share to my inner most thoughts with Him. His friendship was what I really wanted.

As time went on, and I really delved into the Bible I started to ask so many questions about what I was reading. One thing I did was to go to the Lord in prayer numerous times and suggest that since He had made me, He must have had in mind a perfect plan for my life—just as He does for all His children. I suggested that He take my life and do what He wanted with it and in particular apply *HIS* perfect plan to my life. I was just plain tired of trying to run my own life—and not doing a very good job of it either. In addition, I was deeply concerned when reading the part of the Bible that states that broad is the road to hell and many go there but narrow is the road to Heaven and few find it. This was greatly troubling to me—as it should be to you. I prayed to God that if indeed the road is narrow to Heaven than get me to that road.

Matthew 7:13: *Enter ye in at the strait gate: for wide is the gate, and broad is the way, that leadeth to destruction, and many there be which go in thereat*

I think this is a prayer for anyone to pray to Christ. However, be aware that when you give God permission to come into your life and to make changes—lessons you learn most usually involve hardships and sometimes crisis. Many times, we learn our most valuable lessons through the difficult things we go through. "Cushy" lives rarely produce the big life changes that can come from challenging experiences.

After asking God to apply His perfect plan to my life—I believe He honored my request and some amazing things began to happen, as you will soon see…

Deuteronomy 4:29: *But if from thence thou shalt seek the LORD thy God, thou shalt find him, if thou seek him with all thy heart and with all thy soul.*

God's Roses

Every weekday morning, I usually take Ethan to school in my car and one winter morning, a few years ago, seemed the same as any other morning—or so I thought… That morning we piled into our car and it was a cold winter day completely unaware of what we would discover next.

First, we realized that all of our windows were iced over completely. They were covered with what can only be described as extraordinarily similar to solid white-color etched glass windows. The beautiful ice pattern was of *roses—and roses completely covered all the windows.* I can remember exclaiming to Ethan as if it were yesterday—"They're roses—they're roses!" It was just amazing and I have never seen anything like it before or since. All the windows of the car on all sides were decorated with incredibly detailed roses formed on the ice creating solid white-color rose-patterned frozen stained glass windows. *This was one of the most fantastic things I have ever witnessed.* It was indescribable and as if a genius artist had spent hours, detailing lovely roses carved into the ice on every one of our car windows. Tragically, we did not own a digital camera at that time and we had to see the beautiful windows melt away.   I truly feel that only God could have orchestrated such an incredible event for our exclusive benefit.

Song of Solomon 2:1: Beloved
I am the rose of Sharon, and the lily of the valleys.

Job 38:29-30: *Out of whose womb came the ice? And the hoary frost of heaven, who hath gendered it? The waters are hid as with a stone and the face of the deep is frozen.*

Job 37:10: *By the breath of God frost is given: and the breadth of the waters is straitened.*

Chapter Four—I Am Ruined

I Am Ruined

Now I became a Christian when I was very young on my mother's lap and much later on, I recommitted my life to Christ and was formally baptized at my current church. None of these experiences was quite as extraordinary as what happened to me one day in the quiet privacy of my own bedroom.

While alone in my bedroom, I was reading someone else's personal account of the holiness of God. Something about this person's account of God truly convicted me. Even though I did not see any bright lights or anyone at all, suddenly without warning there was an overwhelming presence of God, which I have never experienced before in my life. Without any thought about what I was doing, I threw myself flat on the ground and then I wept and wept with agony and was exceedingly remorseful.

At that point, I caught a small glimpse of the incredible and awesome holiness of God and I simultaneously grasped the horror of my own lack of holiness. I recalled many of the things I had done in my past that had never previously struck me as being any problem or even a big deal. There really are not words to describe the deep anguish I experienced over the realization of my miserable sinful past. I literally felt *that I was ruined*. In addition, these were thoughts that came to my mind—ruination—such ruin—such remorse— regret—utter ruin. I knew I was near a Holy God and there was nothing good about me at all. I despaired greatly over my horribleness. The experience was staggering and I really have no earthly explanation for it. But after such great remorse set in over my horrible past, I felt a great sense of peace—the kind you feel after a storm comes through and the way you feel after the rain has stopped and there is a fresh spring feeling in the air. I felt that kind of incredible peace.

I knew I had an actual encounter with God—but God showed me an event from my distant past. I cannot say for certain if I was given a vision or if it was just brought to mind. This was something I had not thought of for many, many years. When I was a very young girl, my parents would stay for visits at my grandparent's house in Lafayette, Indiana. About two blocks from my grandparent's home was a small church within a very old converted grocery store. I used to walk down to this little church all by myself. Strangely, for a very brief moment, I saw myself walking down a sidewalk going to this church by myself. Even though my parents had Christian parents and were committed Christians later in their lives, they never took me to church while I was young and growing up.

Only God could bring up this memory from my past at that particular moment. I believe that He was letting me know that He was with me even then when I was going to church alone as a young child—*He was with me even then.*

Right after this life-changing encounter with God happened, *without knowing why or how*, I was simply supernaturally led to turn to the verses in **Isaiah 6**. I know for a fact that God directed me to this passage, because at the time I was only interested in reading the New Testament and not the Old Testament at all. I had no foreknowledge about this particular passage in Isaiah and I had no idea why I was directed to turn to this passage. Incredibly, when I read the verse I was amazed by what I read and I absolutely related to Isaiah's experience in this verse where Isaiah describes his utter agony of being in the presence of a holy God as *being ruined.*

Isaiah 6:1-7:

Isaiah's Commission

In the year that king Uzziah died I saw also the LORD sitting upon a throne, high and lifted up, and his train filled the temple. Above it stood the seraphims: each one had six wings; with twain he covered his face, and with twain he covered his feet, and with twain he did fly. And one cried unto another, and said, Holy, holy, holy, is the LORD of hosts: the whole earth is full of his glory. And the posts of the door moved at the voice of him that cried, and the house was filled with smoke. Then said I, Woe is me! For I am undone; because I am a man of unclean lips, and I dwell in the midst of a people of unclean lips: for mine eyes have seen the King, the LORD of hosts. Then flew one of the seraphims unto me, having a live coal in his hand, which he had taken with the tongs from off the altar: And he laid it upon my mouth, and said, Lo, this hath touched thy lips; and thine iniquity is taken away, and thy sin purged.

There was no light in the room; nevertheless, it appeared to me as if it were perfectly light. As I went in and shut the door after me, it seemed to me as if I met the Lord Jesus Christ face-to-face. It did not occur to me then nor did it for some time afterwards, that it was a wholly-mental state. On the contrary, it seemed to me that I saw Him as I would see any other man. He said nothing, but looked at me in such a manner as to break me right down at His feet...it seemed to me a reality that He stood before me and I fell down at His feet and poured out my soul to Him. I wept aloud like a child and made such confessions as I could with a choked utterance. It seemed to me that I bathed His feet with tears, and yet I had no distinct impression that I touched Him.

—Charles Finney, Evangelist

Also, right after this incredible event I know the Lord immediately directed me next to a section of verses in **Hebrews 12:4-11** and I had no explanation why I turned to this passage other than the Lord also led me to it.

Hebrews 12:4-11: *Ye have not yet resisted unto blood, striving against sin. And ye have forgotten the exhortation which speaketh unto you as unto children, My son, despise not thou the chastening of the Lord, nor faint when thou art rebuked of him: For whom the Lord loveth he chasteneth, and scourgeth every son whom he receiveth. If ye endure chastening, God dealeth with you as with sons; for what son is he whom the father chasteneth not? But if ye be without chastisement, whereof all are partakers, then are ye bastards, and not sons. Furthermore we have had fathers of our flesh which corrected us, and we gave them reverence: shall we not much rather be in subjection unto the Father of spirits, and live? For they verily for a few days chastened us after their own pleasure; but he for our profit, that we might be partakers of his holiness. Now no chastening for the present seemeth to be joyous, but grievous: nevertheless afterward it yieldeth the peaceable fruit of righteousness unto them which are exercised thereby.*

I later had an opportunity to share this event within my testimony to my church along with five others who gave their testimonies. I spoke of my feeling of utter and complete ruin and of the change in my heart—shedding anger, bitterness, fear, and more. That day, several people went to the alter to make decisions for Christ after our testimonies. After church when we pulled up in our driveway at home, the car must have been parked in just the right spot (I have never noticed it happening since), because the light hitting our car's side mirror produced a beautiful rainbow on the wall of our stairwell. We opened the door and saw the rainbow up on the wall as we walked through the door. I really believe it was a beautiful sign from God because the Holy Spirit was really with us as we all shared our testimonies at church that morning.

Job 5:17: *Behold, happy is the man whom God correcteth: therefore despise not thou the chastening of the Almighty.*

Prayer of Jabez

Now, not long after these amazing events occurred, I learned about the amazing little story about Jabez, a character in the Bible, whose story takes up a very small space in the Bible, but has a very big message. The prayer of Jabez in the Bible is the following:

1 Chronicles 4:10: *And Jabez called on the God of Israel, saying, Oh that thou wouldest bless me indeed, and enlarge my coast, and that thine hand might be with me, and that thou wouldest keep me from evil, that it may not grieve me! And God granted him that which he requested.*

Many who have prayed this prayer have experienced great blessings from God. I read the prayer and decided to test the prayer. Now at the time, my head was focused on a new business venture I had become involved in, and naively, I thought surely this prayer would be related to my new project. Well as my work plodded along—I wondered if there was really anything to the prayer of Jabez.

I later learned that God does not always bless us with the things we are focused on. I realized because even though my focus was work-oriented, I noticed that I had experienced huge spiritual blessings—not only had God blessed me spiritually, he was even showing me what He had done.

My focus had been on worldly ventures and God had much bigger, long-term blessings in mind. I was humbled and realized the gift God had given me and I felt so shallow that my head had been so caught up in such short-term, temporary pursuits. God's blessing was much better than my little mind could comprehend.

Healing from God

One time, my son Ethan crawled into to our bed in the middle of the night. I knew by just touching him that he was blazing hot. I did not even need to take his temperature. He complained of body aches and chilling. He was on fire with fever and I knew that I was exhausted because it was around 3:00 a.m. I calmly spoke to God this specific simple request, *"As Ethan's caretaker, I would think that You would want me to ask You for help."* At the next exact moment, Ethan's temperature plummeted back down from piping hot to perfectly normal. He suddenly felt normal again and he even said at that moment he felt better right then. It was amazing and there was no time elapsed between Ethan being on fire and the next moment having a normal temperature.

Now I was curious about this incredible experience. The next day, I asked my best friend Beverly, who is a registered nurse; about someone's temperature dropping down like Ethan's did instantaneously. She told me that what happened to Ethan never happens—ever. Temperatures like Ethan's do not just change in one second—they can slowly diminish with time—but they never drop to normal as his did. I know this was an immediate answer to my prayer.

Matthew 8:14-15: *And when Jesus was come into Peter's house, he saw his wife's mother laid, and sick of a fever. And he touched her hand, and the fever left her: and she arose, and ministered unto them.*

John 4:43-54: *Now after two days he departed thence, and went into Galilee. For Jesus himself testified, that a prophet hath no honor in his own country. Then when he was come into Galilee, the Galilaeans received him, having seen all the things that he did at Jerusalem at the feast: for they also went unto the feast. So Jesus came again into Cana of Galilee, where he made the water wine. And there was a certain nobleman, whose son was sick at Capernaum. When he heard that Jesus was come out of Judaea into Galilee, he went unto him, and besought him that he would come down, and heal his son: for he was at the point of death. Then said Jesus unto him, except ye see signs and wonders, ye will not believe. The nobleman saith unto him, Sir, come down here my child die. Jesus saith unto him, Go thy way; thy son liveth. And the man believed the word that Jesus had spoken unto him, and he went his way. And as he was now going down, his servants met him, and told him, saying, Thy son liveth. Then enquired he of them the hour when he began to amend. And they said unto him, yesterday at the seventh hour the fever left him. So the father knew that it was at the same hour, in the which Jesus said unto him, Thy son liveth: and himself believed, and his whole house. This is again the second miracle that Jesus did, when he was come out of Judaea into Galilee.*

Another time, I was experiencing incredible pain in my head all day and I had been taking pain medicine all day for it. I called my best friend (a nurse) Beverly and she did not know what was causing it at the time either. It felt as if an ice pick was being stabbed into the side of my head. The next day, I had to go to my mother's place and on the way; I realized that I had left without taking some more medicine for the pain, because I was in such a hurry. I was aggravated with myself for forgetting the medicine and my head was still hurting in the same place. I put my hand on my head where it was hurting and I asked God if He would help me with my hurting head. Therefore, after I prayed immediately, a thought came into my mind that was not my own and it was, "*You have a pinched nerve and you need to stretch*"—so I did stretch and it went completely away as quickly as I had asked for help.

Apple of My Eye

One morning my husband had left a bowl of sliced apples on the table before heading out for work and he never does this—NEVER. I was reading a book about someone's near-death experience at the time and how they happened to be taken by God to Heaven during the Jewish holiday Rosh Hashanah. They talked about how in Heaven everyone celebrates this holiday by eating apples and honey. So here is the most amazing thing—that day I happened to turn randomly (with no foreknowledge) to this amazing account, and *it actually was Rosh Hashanah that very day*. And I should just happen to turn exactly to this part in this book about Rosh Hashanah and about celebrating with apples and there just happened to be a bowl of sliced apples my husband left on the table? So I did the only thing I could do, I got up and got some honey and tried eating apples with honey. It was a surreal moment and it was as if this moment were prepared by God for me to celebrate Rosh Hashanah.

Chapter Five—Ask and Ye Shall Receive

Ask and Ye Shall Receive

One evening, my husband Steve and I were coming from a meeting and we both were starving so we decided to stop at a restaurant. Now we were the only ones waiting to be seated up front and not far from us were not one, but even two waitresses, nearby where we were standing. We waited as these waitresses flitted around, from one table to the next, seemingly completely oblivious that we were standing waiting for a table within a few feet of them. My husband finally said that he was tired of waiting and we should go. However, I insisted to wait. We waited some more and the servers who were so near us, never even acknowledged we were there. It was strange and it was as if we were invisible. Therefore, we agreed to leave and go eat somewhere else.

We went to another restaurant nearby and the host gave us a table quickly. Now, I also want to mention that two days prior I moved a stack of Bibles in my dining room to my car trunk. I just wanted them out of the dining room. That night at the restaurant, for some reason, I decided to bring my own Bible to the table. After dinner, our server came to our table and exclaimed, "Oh, I see you read the Bible." I thought, "Well okay" and then she said that *just that day* she learned that she had leukemia and she was the single mother to two young children. She then asked us if we would pray for her.

Well we did pray for her and I asked for her phone number so I could stay in touch with her and pray for her. So we swapped phone numbers. I also asked her if she would like a Bible too, that I just happened to have an extra one in my car (remember the Bibles I put in my trunk from my dining room?). She said she would like to have one and so I gave her one to keep.

Now on the way home, Steve was saying that he thought it was strange how the servers at the first restaurant just refused to seat us even though we were close to them—they did not even act as if they saw us. Moreover, he thought the whole thing was amazingly coincidental. *I told him that just that morning I had prayed to God that I was not very good at approaching people, but if He wanted to send someone my way, then I would talk to them.*

The next day I called the number, the young woman had given me and her grandmother answered. Now the grandmother, a God-fearing woman, said that she was praying that God would send someone to help her granddaughter.

About the time I had helped the waitress, I spoke of earlier in this account—and I still pray for her almost daily—I experienced the worst satanic attack. I began to believe (in error) that I had committed the unforgivable sin of blaspheming the Holy Spirit probably at one point in my life and I believed that I must be forever doomed. I was carrying this burden for a few weeks—I was sick and beside myself with the lowest grief, I have ever experienced—personal separation from the Lord. I even discovered that Billy Graham's own father went through this same personal torture one time. I tried to read books about the Holy Spirit to console myself—but I never felt completely assured.

My son is part of a puppet ministry team and the group was going to a festival at Olivette University in Illinois. During a Saturday morning chapel service, about 300 people who were there for this festival had gathered to hear the minister who gave a very Spirit-filled message. In the middle of this service, the man stopped cold and looked out in the audience and said that he had a message for someone here who believes they committed the unforgivable sin. He proceeded to say *that if that had happened that you would not be at this festival*. Then he proceeded again with his message as if nothing had happened.

I was dumbfounded—and I wondered it that message was for me—but I claimed it as my own and found the relief that I so desired when I could not find it any other way. I can hardly write this copy without crying about the extreme anguish I experienced at the thought of being forever separated from God and the extreme relief from knowing that God was still with me. I wonder how awful it is that so many people set themselves up to be separated from God for eternity and my soul aches knowing this is happening to people all the time. I cannot stress enough the importance of seeking God in this life while you still can and not putting Christ on the back burner of your life.

Now I have since learned that the young woman I met at the restaurant, whom I prayed for, did have her leukemia go into remission and has since become much better. Many people I knew were praying for her. Much later, I went back to the Evangelism committee of my church and I asked them if we could create an outreach challenge and ask the church to pray the same prayer I did on that one morning I met the young woman from the restaurant. *I challenged them to pray: I know I am not too good about approaching people, but that if the Lord wanted to send someone my way, I would be willing to talk to them.* I knew I wanted to purchase enough Bibles to provide to our entire church congregation to do the outreach challenge and that was going to require at least $600. The committee was behind the effort, so I next went to our church pastor who was behind the effort but suggested that we wait until the new fiscal year to purchase the needed Bibles. I did not want to fold so quickly on doing the outreach in the current fiscal year, so I sincerely prayed to God for the needed money. The period was during some of the worst announcements of economic disaster by the media. Everyone was concerned about the economic state of affairs. Incredibly and miraculously, God delivered $600 within 24 to 48 hours of my prayer request for the Bible outreach challenge. While some of the worst economic news was being announced in the news, God was delivering to me $600 on short notice for a Bible outreach challenge!

Right away, I returned to my church pastor and told him that I had prayed for the money to purchase Bibles for the entire church for the Bible outreach challenge. I told him I received enough money to purchase New Testaments for the entire church and I did not think God wanted us to wait to do the challenge. My pastor agreed and moved the challenge back into the current year. I was able to make the challenge to the entire church and to handout Bibles to everyone in the sanctuary. God is not necessarily looking for a bunch of outreach heroes as much as He is looking for people who are openly willing to allow God to use them however He desires. Please take the challenge today and pray: *"Lord, I am not too good at approaching people, but if you send someone my way, I would be willing to talk to them."*

Lord Send Me

God had immediately honored my request to reach out to someone in need when I told God I was available *on that very day*—this was not the last time God would grant such a request. There was another time in which I told God that I was willing and available to speak to others about God, if He wanted to use me. *Within 24 hours of making this plea to God*, I had not one, but *two* speaking engagements to two different groups. This is not normally something I ever do either. It was incredible.

A very dear friend of mine had invited me to come to a Bible study group with her where several different professional people gather for breakfast and Bible discussions. During my visit, I made a few comments about some of my personal experiences with God and the person in charge of the study came up to me and declared that I would be their speaker within the next two weeks. It happened just as they described, I came back and spoke of my testimony and experiences with God to this group of seekers.

The second occurrence was just as dizzying as the first. I had made an appointment to speak to my church pastor about church evangelism. Prior to going in to the church for my meeting I prayed that if God wanted to use me to speak to the church that I would wait for an invitation from our pastor and if I received no invitation, then I would know that it was not in God's will and I would not pursue speaking at the church. After a few minutes of discussing some of the exciting things that the Lord was doing in my life, our pastor asked me how He could encourage others in the church to pursue such a relationship with the Lord. I took this cue and simply asked if I could speak to them—and the pastor did not hesitate but said he would be glad for me to speak to the church on a Sunday evening and so he wrote me into the schedule to give the entire Sunday night service within a month of our meeting. A month later, I found myself in front of a group of people once again giving my testimony. *This was the second of two speaking engagements within 24 to 48 hours of letting God know I was available to speak to groups.* You will never know what God can do in your life unless you make yourself available to Him.

Incredible Coincidences?

Proverbs 8:17: *I love them that love me; and those that seek me early shall find me.*

After surrendering to Christ and intensely seeking God, I began to notice a plethora of incredible occurrences that are so amazing I could only believe that God has been demonstrating His awesome abilities. After relentlessly going after God and believing that His friendship was attainable (because He asks us for ours), I was inspired by the things I started to notice happening to me frequently. I say that I sought His friendship and some may think that this an arrogant claim on my part, but through reading the Bible I was shown that Jesus said the most important commandment is **Deuteronomy 6:5:** *And thou shalt love the LORD thy God with all thine heart, and with all thy soul, and with all thy might.* I am pressed to comprehend how you love God first without devoting much time to that pursuit and somehow simultaneously suppressing the idea of friendship. This seems impossible to me.

The other requests I had made to God was for Him to take my life from me—the life He had given me in the first place—and from it, apply His own perfect plan for the life He had originally created. Laying down my life in complete surrender included giving over my fears. Fears come from the lack of knowing the future and a feeling of lack of control over that unknown future that leads to fearfulness. In turning to my faith by deciding to turn over fears for the future to God then I experienced a major release of pain and frustration. Entrusting all the outcomes of the future into the hands of Jesus and replacing unwarranted worries and anguish to His capable hands gave me immediate relief from all future fears to come. God was more than capable of dealing with my personal worries. I just had but to admit that I could no longer carry the burden on my own. Jesus says in **Matthew 11:30:** *"For my yoke is easy, and my burden is light."*

Because my fears and control of my own life was what I surrendered to the Lord, I believe that He in turn did something amazing and miraculous in my life. He demonstrated to me His phenomenal abilities and control over everything—every detail of our lives. When I began to see these unbelievable things taking place, at first of course I was in denial that they were anything but amazing coincidences happening. Then the more frequently they took place the more I started to begin to get past the idea that this was all some coincidence. I was also becoming closer to Christ. When many amazing things began to happen, I then believed *in my heart* that God was showing me just how powerful He is and how comprehensive His reach is into the incredible details of our lives. I began to realize how God even concerns Himself with the minute details of our lives. The revelation of this truth for me personally was that God really has control of all the little circumstances and cares about the tiniest events of our lives. He knows all about these things and intervenes on our behalf.

All the things that happened indicated to me that God is in control of what is happening in my life at every moment. This has been very comforting and a relief to realize that God does care so much about every single small detail and that He loves us all the time. What an assurance I have found that God's human network of control is huge and He can bring together any person or any circumstance in your life for your benefit when you put all your trust in Him. Sometimes this can mean providing you with comfort or support and sometimes it can mean assigning you with great difficulty, which later may lead to learning about God and His ways.

Life as a surrendered Christian is a journey that can lead to shorter paths but many times the very best way can lead through rocky terrain where you learn the most and draw the nearest to Christ. Surrendering your life and all to Christ can be a matter of perspective. Many people in the beginning enter into surrender reluctantly and find this to be a great undertaking—as if they are conceding their personal freedoms and human rights. When Christians have come to the feet of Christ to surrender all—it is often times after hitting absolute bottom and trying all other possible human scenarios and failings. These failures can be with personal relationships, finances, health problems, addictions of all kinds, fears, depression, and self-idolatry to name a few.

In the beginning, when I finally conceded for Christ to take control of my life it was a relief but not until I had struggled under my own strength to attempt to conquer my fears and frustrations with life. At the point I began to see my feeble attempts to control my life as fatally futile is when I threw my hands in the air and cried, "Enough—Lord take this burden from me!"

These days though, my daily surrender is to my dearest and best friend in the world whom I have grown to know and trust with all my being. In addition, daily surrender has turned the corner from a painful and deliberate fight to give up "self" over to Christ to a race to give myself to Him joyfully. I now celebrate that He will take my life and run it for me. Walking with the One who loves us like no one else ever will makes daily surrender look as if we are giving in to leaving a cold padded cell to land on a goose down silk comforter with a warm robe, fluffy slippers, a hot cup of cocoa with whipped cream. You start to think, "What was I thinking?—surrendering to Christ was the best thing for me—why was I formerly so stubborn about this most wonderful decision?"

So the following are some accounts of the incredible events that I began to notice happening to me following my surrendering to Christ and asking Him to apply *His* perfect plan to my life…

Chapter Six—I Chose You

I Chose You

Many times, I would be home alone and talking to God and one day excitedly, I so happily (and naively) exclaimed that, "*I was glad that I HAD CHOSEN GOD.*" Now after I made this giant statement, *THE VERY NEXT THING I DID*, I strolled right into my kitchen and next I threw open the Bible that was sitting on my kitchen table. I randomly looked straight down on the page I opened to *AND MY EYES FIRST FELL* on these words that jumped off the page at me—*"I CHOSE YOU."* I was in utter shock, amazement, and simultaneously in awe and humbled by this event. In fact, I nearly fell over at the sight of these words in response to my saying *I was glad I had chosen God.* With the number of words in the average Bible numbering 774,746, this demonstrates just how incredible and improbable that I would open to the exact location of these words and look at these particular words on that page, and it completely puts the event in its miraculous perspective.

So what exactly was God trying to tell me? I had declared that I was so glad that I had chosen Him only to turn around a minute later to lay open the Bible and look down at the words: "I CHOSE YOU." So did I choose God first—or did He choose me first? Do we choose God or does God first choose us?

Jesus says we are literally nothing without Him. There is nothing good in us apart from God. How could men empty of God even value God enough to come to Him? They cannot. God is in complete control of everything—He is omniscient, omnipresent, and sovereign. Would God really be so sovereign if He stood back and waited as men controlled destiny by choosing for God or against God? Would not all destinies be altered by which men became Christian and which men did not? What if someone like Billy Graham had not become a Christian—what has been the impact of that one life to others? Would God, who is utterly sovereign and all-powerful, really step aside and wait to see if men would come to Him or not? In addition, just how can men, who are completely devoid of goodness apart from God and evil from birth, find the answers needed within themselves apart from God, to choose God? Let us allow the Bible to speak for itself on this matter of whether man chooses God or whether God chooses man.

I have given this a lot of thought about God choosing us. So many people believe they choose God first. However, is this really the case? We know that God is sovereign, omniscient, omnipotent, and in complete control… So do we really believe that God would leave so much control in the hands of His creation? Let us look at this further—one man comes to Christ, then He leads several more to Christ. So what if that one man did not choose Christ? What happens to the other people? Does the clay really control the outcome of the potter's plan?

Many people believe that God chooses men because He looks down the corridor of time and sees which men will choose Him and who will not. So God bases His decisions on what He sees men doing in the future? We are still placing control of the future on men in this scenario.

God consequently foretells the future because He plans and controls the future. The Bible says that God gave His Son to be crucified for us. God was in control of this event. Jesus chose the 12 disciples and God was in control. So exactly what are men in control of? Well according to the Bible, certainly not even making plans for ourselves into the future for such things as doing business or planning for a profit is considered evil according to **James 4:13-16**.

James 4:13-16: *Go to now, ye that say, Today or tomorrow we will go into such a city, and continue there a year, and buy and sell, and get gain: Whereas ye know not what shall be on the morrow. For what is your life? It is even a vapor that appeareth for a little time, and then vanisheth away. For that ye ought to say, If the Lord will, we shall live, and do this, or that. But now ye rejoice in your boastings: all such rejoicing is evil.*

The Bible says God chose men before the foundation of the world in a predestined plan. Let us look at the following verses from the Bible:

Ephesians 1:4-5: *According as he hath chosen us in him before the foundation of the world, that we should be holy and without blame before him in love: Having predestinated us unto the adoption of children by Jesus Christ to himself, according to the good pleasure of his will,*

1 Peter 1:20: *Who verily was foreordained before the foundation of the world, but was manifest in these last times for you.*

Acts 13:48: *And when the Gentiles heard this, they were glad, and glorified the word of the Lord: and as many as were ordained to eternal life believed.*

John 15:18-19: *If the world hates you, ye know that it hated me before it hated you. If ye were of the world, the world would love his own: but because ye are not of the world, but I have chosen you out of the world, therefore the world hateth you.*

Let's look at **Exodus 10:1-2:** *And the LORD said unto Moses, **Go in unto Pharaoh: for I have hardened his heart, and the heart of his servants, that I might shew these my signs before him:** And that thou mayest tell in the ears of thy son, and of thy son's son, what things I have wrought in Egypt, and my signs which I have done among them; that ye may know how that I am the LORD.*

And, we can look at **Exodus 7:3-4:** ***And I will harden Pharaoh's heart,*** *and multiply my signs and my wonders in the land of Egypt. But Pharaoh shall not hearken unto you, that I may lay my hand upon Egypt, and bring forth mine armies, and my people the children of Israel, out of the land of Egypt by great judgments.*

In these two passages from the Old Testament, we see despite the horrible plagues brought on Egypt, God had hardened Pharaoh's heart and even though the choice would seem to be an easy one—*for Pharaoh to make*—God chose for Pharaoh not to acknowledge God for God's own purposes.

So does God choose men because He can foresee what men will do in the future? The Bible says specifically **all** men are an enmity to God and have their backs turned against God. Therefore, God foresees down the corridors of time all men as initially evil apart from Him. Only when he draws men as He chooses and *gives them His spirit,* can they turn to Christ and be saved through Jesus' provision of justification for evil men through the cross. Let us look at these two verses:

Romans 3:23: *For all have sinned, and come short of the glory of God;*

Isaiah 53:6: *All we like sheep have gone astray; we have turned everyone to his own way; and the LORD hath laid on him the iniquity of us all.*

In addition, the Bible outlines that *without the Spirit of God,* the natural man cannot *see* or *turn* to God.

Ephesians 2:1-5: *And you hath he quickened, who were dead in trespasses and sins; Wherein in time past ye walked according to the course of this world, according to the prince of the power of the air, the spirit that now worketh in the children of disobedience: Among whom also we all had our conversation in times past in the lusts of our flesh, fulfilling the desires of the flesh and of the mind; and were by nature the children of wrath, even as others. But God, who is rich in mercy, for his great love wherewith he loved us, Even when we were dead in sins, hath quickened us together with Christ, (by grace ye are saved).*

Jesus says that only God is good and men are completely devoid of what it takes to turn to Christ, unless God draws them to Himself.

Romans 3:11-12: *There is none that understandeth, there is none that seeketh after God. They are all gone out of the way, they are together become unprofitable; there is none that doeth good, no, not one.*

1 Corinthians 1:21: *For after that in the wisdom of God the world by wisdom knew not God, it pleased God by the foolishness of preaching to save them that believe.*

Ezekiel 11:19: *And I will give them one heart, and I will put a new spirit within you; and I will take the stony heart out of their flesh, and will give them an heart of flesh:*

Unless the Father draws men to His Son Christ, they will not turn to Him. Natural man cannot turn to God on his own apart from God.

Here are some more corresponding verses:

John 6:44: Jesus said: *No man can come to me, except the Father which hath sent me draw him: and I will raise him up at the last day.*

1 Corinthians 12:3: *Wherefore I give you to understand, that no man speaking by the Spirit of God calleth Jesus accursed: and that no man can say that Jesus is the Lord, but by the Holy Ghost.*

Acts 16:14: *And a certain woman named Lydia, a seller of purple, of the city of Thyatira, which worshipped God, heard us: **whose heart the Lord opened,** that she attended unto the things which were spoken of Paul.*

John 6:63-65: *Is the spirit that quickeneth; the flesh profiteth nothing: the words that I speak unto you, they are spirit and they are life. But there are some of you that believe not. For Jesus knew from the beginning who they were that believed unto, and who should betray him. And he said, therefore said I unto you, that no man can come unto me, except it were given unto him of my Father.*

Romans 5:8: *But God commendeth his love toward us, in that, while we were yet sinners, Christ died for us.*

*The father loves the child when the child does not know the father, much less love him. It is the same with us (**1 John 4:10:** Herein is love, not that we loved God, but that he loved us, and sent his Son to be the propitiation for our sins).*
*We are, by nature, 'haters of God' (**Romans 1:29-32:** Being filled with all unrighteousness, fornication, wickedness, covetousness, maliciousness; full of envy, murder, debate, deceit, malignity; whisperers, Backbiters, haters of God, despiteful, proud, boasters, inventors of evil things, disobedient to parents, Without understanding, covenant breakers, without natural affection, implacable, unmerciful: Who knowing the judgment of God, that they which commit such things are worthy of death, not only do the same, but have pleasure in them that do them).*
God in His own nature is a lover of men. Therefore, God's love must precede ours.

Our love responds to God's love. No sinner ever turned his heart to God if the heart of God were not first set on the sinner. God must be revealed to us as lovely, desirable, as a fit and suitable object of rest to the soul, before we can ever love God.

~John Owen

John 6:35-39: *And Jesus said unto them, I am the bread of life: he that cometh to me shall never hunger; and he that believeth on me shall never thirst. But I said unto you, that ye also have seen me, and believe not. All that the Father giveth me shall come to me; and him that cometh to me I will in no wise cast out.*

For I came down from heaven, not to do mine own will, but the will of him that sent me. And this is the Father's will which hath sent me, that of all which he hath given me I should lose nothing, but should raise it up again at the last day.

God, the Father, draws men to His Son's salvation or men are completely incapable of getting there on their own. Without this gift of God drawing men to Christ and Himself—men would be lost in their sins.

Romans 9:11-23: *For the children being not yet born, neither having done any good or evil, that the purpose of God according to the election might stand, not of works, but of him that calleth. It was said unto her, The elder shall serve the younger. As it was written, Jacob have I loved, but Esau have I hated. What shall I say then? Is there unrighteousness with God? God forbid. For he saith to Moses, I will have mercy on whom I will have mercy, and I will have compassion on whom I will have compassion. So then it is not of him that willeth, nor him that runneth but of God that sheweth mercy. For the scripture saith unto Pharaoh, even for this same purpose have I raised thee up, that I might shew my power in thee, and that my name might be declared throughout all the earth therefore hath he mercy on whom he will have mercy and whom he will he hardeneth. Though wilt say then unto me, why doth he yet find fault? For who hath resisted his will? Nay but, O man, who art thou that repliest against God. Shall the thing formed say to him that formed it, Why hast thou made me thus? Hath not the potter power over the clay, of the same lump to make one vessel unto honor, and another unto dishonor? What if God, willing to shew his wrath, and to make his power known, endured with much longsuffering the vessels of wrath fitted to destruction: And that he might make known the riches of his glory on the vessels of mercy, which he had afore prepared unto glory.*

Proverbs: 16:4: *The LORD hath made all things for himself: yea, even the wicked for the day of evil.*

Philippians 1:6: *Being confident of this very thing, that he which hath begun a good work in you will perform it until the day of Jesus Christ:*

If men could choose God and work for their salvation then they could boast about choosing God and God would not be in total control of everything. And, salvation therefore would not actually be the free merciful gift of grace that it truly is if men could boast about choosing. If men could choose, they would boast.

1 Corinthians 18-31: *For the preaching of the cross is to them that perish foolishness; but unto us who are saved it is the power of God. For it is written, I will destroy the wisdom of the wise, and will bring to nothing the understanding of the prudent. Where is the wise? Where is the scribe? Where is the disputer of this world? Hath not God made foolish the wisdom of this world? For after that in the wisdom of God the world by wisdom knew not God, it pleased God by the foolishness of preaching to save them that believe. For the Jews require a sign, and the Greeks seek after wisdom: But we preach Christ crucified, unto the Jews a stumbling block, and unto the Greeks foolishness; But unto them which are called, both Jews and Greeks, Christ the power of God, and the wisdom of God. Because the foolishness of God is wiser than men; and the weakness of God is stronger than men. For ye see your calling, brethren, how that not many wise men after the flesh, not many mighty, not many noble, are called: But God hath chosen the foolish things of the world to confound the wise; and God hath chosen the weak things of the world to confound the things which are mighty; And base things of the world, and things which are despised, hath God chosen, yea, and things which are not, to bring to nought things that are: That no flesh should glory in his presence. But of him are ye in Christ Jesus, who of God is made unto us wisdom, and righteousness, and sanctification, and redemption: That, according as it is written, He that glorieth, let him glory in the Lord.*

Ephesians 2:9-10: *Not of works, lest any man should boast. For we are his workmanship, created in Christ Jesus unto good works, which God hath before ordained that we should walk in them.*

Psalms 139:16: *Thine eyes did see my substance, yet being imperfect; and in thy book all my members were written, which in continuance were fashioned, when as yet there was none of them.*

Matthew 24:31: *And he shall send his angels with a great sound of a trumpet, and they shall gather together his elect from the four winds, from one end of heaven to the other.*

Romans 8:28-33: *And we know that all things work together for good to them that love God, to them who are the called according to his purpose. For whom he did foreknow, he also did predestinate to be conformed to the image of his Son, that he might be the firstborn among many brethren. Moreover whom he did predestinate, them he also called: and whom he called, them he also justified: and whom he justified, them he also glorified. What shall we then say to these things? If God be for us, who can be against us? He that spared not his own Son, but delivered him up for us all, how shall he not with him also freely give us all things. Who shall lay anything to the charge of God's elect? It is God that justifieth.*

Mark 13:20: *And except that the Lord had shortened those days, no flesh should be saved: but for the elect's sake, whom he hath chosen, he hath shortened the days.*

Romans 11:5-8: *Even so then at this present time also there is a remnant according to the election of grace. And if by grace then is it no more of works: otherwise grace is no more grace. But if it be of works, then it is no more grace: otherwise work is no more work. What then? Israel hath not obtained that which he seeketh for; but the election hath obtained it, and the rest were blinded. (According as it is written, God hath given them the spirit of slumber, eyes that they should not see, and ears that they should not hear;) unto this day.*

2 Peter 1:3-4: *According as his divine power hath given unto us all things that pertain unto life and godliness, **through the knowledge of him that hath called us to glory and virtue:** Whereby are given unto us exceeding great and precious promises: that by these ye might be partakers of the divine nature, having escaped the corruption that is in the world through lust.*

Revelation 17:14: *These shall make war with the Lamb, and the Lamb shall overcome them: for he is Lord of lords, and King of kings: **and they that are with him are called, and chosen, and faithful.***

Finally, **1 Peter 1-2** says it all perfectly:

1 Peter 1-2: *Peter, an apostle of Jesus Christ, to the strangers scattered throughout Pontus, Galatia, Cappadocia, Asia, and Bithynia, Elect according to the foreknowledge of God the Father, through sanctification of the Spirit, unto obedience and sprinkling of the blood of Jesus Christ: Grace unto you, and peace, be multiplied.*

One way to see this is the Bible clearly shows that apart from Christ we are nothing. In addition, if you think man in the flesh can choose God although man is supposedly making this decision while completely deplete of the Spirit of God, the Bible shows this as being impossible. Otherwise then man could boast that he was capable of choosing God on his own while completely apart and devoid of God's Spirit.

One final comment about this matter is that the Bible throughout illustrates the relationship between Jesus, the Son of God, and the church is as a bride marrying her groom. When Christ is united with His people who He saves, it is like a marriage relationship in the tradition of Jewish marriage customs. In Jewish marriage customs, the father chooses the bride for the son. The bride never chooses.

In my former state of arrogance, I believed wrongly that I chose God and God set me straight. I cannot take any credit for initially pursuing God and I cannot admit to being so clever or brilliant to make such a choice on my own. Had God not pursued me, I would have surely been lost and alienated from God. **All I can boast about is God's incredible mercy and amazing grace for a desperate lost sinner like me!**

Chapter Seven—Those Amazing Wonders & Signs

Zechariah

One time while I was home, I was reading a verse online on my computer randomly from Zechariah—I turned off my computer and then I went downstairs for lunch and decided to open the Bible randomly and read something. I then opened up the Bible arbitrarily and looked down and I went to the *exact* verse I had just read a few minutes earlier online in Zechariah. What specifically are the odds of that happening? It was amazing. (Remember there are 774,746 words in the average Bible.)

Don't Be Like a Horse...

One day, I was talking to God and feeling badly about an argument I had with my husband and I admitted to God that I was like a wild horse that sometimes needed to be reined in. The VERY NEXT THING I DID after this conversation with God was go to Bible verses online on my computer and the exact next verse that literally popped up was *"Don't be like a horse that needs to be bridled..."* Now, I actually almost fell over from shock when this verse came up randomly on my computer right after admitting that I was just like a wild horse that needed to be reined in—incredible. Yes, I believe God has a glorious sense of humor. Do you remember the story in the Bible about Sarah when God tells her that she will have a baby in her old age and she laughs with disbelief? **Genesis 21:6-7** says: *And Sarah said, God hath made me to laugh, so that all that hear will laugh with me. And she said, Who would have said unto Abraham, that Sarah should have given children suck? For I have born him a son in his old age.*

Psalms 32:9: *Be ye not as the horse, or as the mule, which have no understanding: whose mouth must be held in with bit and bridle, lest they come near unto thee.*

Bread Alone

Matthew 4:4: *But he answered and said, It is written, Man shall not live by bread alone, but by every word that proceedeth out of the mouth of God.*

In an effort to fit more time for God into my busy schedule, I stopped watching television during lunchtime and spent my time reading my Bible instead. One day, during this special time with God over lunch, I was holding a piece of bread with one hand and the Bible I was reading with the other hand. As I picked up the bread and was about to take a bite, I glanced over at a verse in the Bible completely at random and my eyes fell on these words: "Man does not live on bread alone." I almost fell out of my chair.

In the past, I gave so little time and consideration to God. I used to think that church on Sunday and an activity at church was good enough. The Bible was difficult to understand at best. God was...*in my mind*...consigned to a specific block of time, only to be released during certain hours of the week and whenever I needed something from Him. Other things that I thought were more important (although not really) selfishly filled my days and all the things I believed would give me greater control over my own life.

But, after I became interested in my personal research of Heaven, I read much about the devotion of His true followers. It seemed that the message was always clear to *Love the Lord God above all else.* How do you do that if you never give Him any of your time I wondered? I took inventory of my life and I had truly failed in this department. Finding time for God became an utmost priority to me and my desire was not driven from duty or some other cold and rigid compulsion. This was different—it was from my interest in expressing love to a God who had bothered to make and care for me and for Christ His Son who bothered to come to earth and die to save me. It was also to begin establishing a relationship and to know God better Who with I wanted to spend eternity. In addition, the question for me has been "Just Who is this person we will be spending eternity with and worshipping?"…"Why am I waiting to get to know Him?"…"What does this all mean to me?" Therefore, I wanted to strategize on finding ways to spend time with God and I really put forth effort to find ways to communicate with Him and learn more about Him within the time constraints of my busy daily schedule.

Lunchtime was a great place to eliminate unnecessary time wasters and find time to read my Bible. There was also all that wasted time driving on errands listening to the radio—so that became one of the best times for me to talk to God during all my hours of commuting around. Strangely, the more time I spent with God, the more I valued these special times. I really wanted to dedicate more time to God that I believed He deserved. After all, He had given me so very much to be thankful for and my interest in focusing on God grew. Again, this did not seem like a chore to me—but a growing focused interest.

God is always available to any one of us when we look for Him—He will be found. **Deuteronomy 4:29** says *But if from thence thou shalt seek the LORD thy God, thou shalt find him, if thou seek him with all thy heart and with all thy soul.* This is absolute, unquestionable truth from God Himself. The Holy Spirit is patient and He wants you to seek Him out and **Matthew 7:7** says, *Ask, and it shall be given you; seek, and ye shall find; knock, and it shall be opened unto you:*

Jesus: The Good Shepherd
My sincere belief was that whether I ever heard back from God or not, I still owed it to Him to spend time with Him. He gave me so much—my life, my salvation, my daily needs, and hopefully a future with Him. Honestly, I was not counting on God communicating back with me in any form and I did not really expect hearing from Him in any way. I was never looking for anything to happen because I pursued Him.

The Bible proved accurate to me that when you sincerely seek God *you will find Him.* **Hebrews 11:6** says: *But without faith it is impossible to please him: for he that cometh to God must believe that he is, and that he is a rewarder of them that diligently seek him.* In my heart, I really wanted God to know that I cared for Him and that He was worth pursing and seeking.

One of the most incredible occurrences I had was after praying. I prayed a most, unique prayer one evening—in a way I normally never pray. *In this prayer, I thought of Christ as the Good Shepherd and that I just wanted Him to put me over His shoulders like a sheep and for Him to carry me to safety.* After praying this prayer, I put my son Ethan to bed and the next thing I did was to read to my son from his abbreviated Bible stories for kids. Without having any clue as to what story was coming up next in his book, I read a couple short stories and *the third one was about the Good Shepherd who puts the lamb over His shoulder to carry it to safety.* This amazed me—what were the chances that I would pray the same thing I would read about a few minutes later. Only the Holy Spirit could arrange this experience. I was just beginning to learn about the unique ways the Holy Spirit communicates with us.

Here is the Bible story I read to my son that night after I had prayed to Christ that I wanted to be like a lamb He carried on His shoulder to safety:

Luke 15:1-7: The Parable of the Lost Sheep
Then drew near unto him all the publicans and sinners for to hear him. And the Pharisees and scribes murmured, saying, This man receiveth sinners, and eateth with them. And he spake this parable unto them, saying, What man of you, having an hundred sheep, if he lose one of them, doth not leave the ninety and nine in the wilderness, and go after that which is lost, until he find it? And when he hath found it, he layeth it on his shoulders, rejoicing. And when he cometh home, he calleth together his friends and neighbors, saying unto them, rejoice with me; for I have found my sheep which was lost. I say unto you, that likewise joy shall be in heaven over one sinner that repenteth, more than over ninety and nine just persons, which need no repentance.

Cinnamon

Yet another amazing thing happened to me one day when I was home eating lunch alone. I just decided I needed cinnamon for something I was eating. I so rarely ever use cinnamon that it was probably the first I had gone to my cabinet to look for it in a very long time. I had to search for it in our cabinet and I was not even sure we had any cinnamon on hand. After finding it, I thought about how cinnamon was a spice mentioned in the Bible. While I was eating, I opened the devotional study guide I had been reading and at the bottom of the page, I had been reading I came to this section after turning to the next page:

The section I was reading also included the Bible's meaning for cinnamon. It amazed me that I should be using cinnamon and wondering what the Biblical significance of **cinnamon** was only to next turn to the section in a book I was reading about cinnamon.

Song of Solomon 14:13-14: *Thy plants are an orchard of pomegranates, with pleasant fruits; camphire, with spikenard, Spikenard and saffron; calamus and **cinnamon**, with all trees of frankincense; myrrh and aloes, with all the chief spices:*

Praise God in the Storms

Lately I have had many times listening to things on the radio or TV playing in the background and while also reading the words in the Bible simultaneously. For instance, we had the radio playing a song I heard all about praising God in the Storms of life and as I heard this, I opened the Bible and I looked down and completely randomly I came to the section talking about *Jesus calming the storm*.

We go to God for things we need (or think we need) and solutions to our problems. God is fine with this as long as what we ask for is within "His will." When you pray, you need to ask if what you are praying for would be in God's will—owning a new sports car may not be in His will for instance. We need to pray for others and for personal guidance. We need to pray for repentance of all our sins and to search us for sins we may not easily see in ourselves. But when things are not going our way and things may be falling apart around us—are we praising God in our prayers? Are we praising Him in the storms? Are we thanking Him when He calms our storms?

God is completely worthy of praise and thanksgiving before, during, and after the storms of our lives. We owe God so much of our praise for our very existence and His unfailing love and care throughout our lives. We owe God praise for what He will do in our futures that we cannot even see right now. Let us never grow tired of giving God the praise He is due, even through the storms.

Matthew 8:23-27: *And when he was entered into a ship, his disciples followed him. And, behold, there arose a great tempest in the sea, insomuch that the ship was covered with the waves: but he was asleep. And his disciples came to him, and awoke him, saying, Lord, save us: we perish. And he saith unto them, Why are ye fearful, O ye of little faith? Then he arose, and rebuked the winds and the sea; and there was a great calm. But the men marveled, saying, what manner of man is this, that even the winds and the sea obey him!*

Putting on the Armor

In an effort to fill vacancies of my day with time with God, I have found that one of the very best times to meet Him is during all the running around in the car I do when I am alone. This is one of the very best times to communicate with God because there can be a lot of downtime while running around alone in the car. During one of these morning trip times with my usual conversation with God going on, I talked to Him all about **the armor of God and that I wanted to put on the helmet of salvation, the breastplate of righteousness, the belt of truth, and the shield of faith**. Now I want to add that this is probably the first time I have ever said such a thing. Not long after that, I came home and opened my email messages for the morning and I was once again astonished at what I saw. The email devotion I received was all about putting on the armor of God.

Here is the actual verse about the armor of God from the Bible I opened to in my morning email:

Ephesians 6:11-17: *Put on the whole armor of God, which ye may be able to stand against the wiles of the devil. For we wrestle not against flesh and blood, but against principalities, against powers, against the rulers of the darkness of this world, against spiritual wickedness in high places. Wherefore take unto you the whole armor of God that ye may be able to withstand in the evil day, and having done all, to stand. Stand therefore, having your loins girt about with truth, and having on the breastplate of righteousness; And your feet shod with the preparation of the gospel of peace; Above all, taking the shield of faith, wherewith ye shall be able to quench all the fiery darts of the wicked. And take the helmet of salvation, and the sword of the Spirit, which is the word of God:*

Lying to Others

One day we were at our family cabin. I had forgotten that it was not a good plan to plug in my laptop on the same wall the microwave was plugged into. Well I blew the breaker and my husband Steve asked me pointblank if I had done it. Unfortunately, my knee jerk reaction was to outright lie and say, "No" because I felt so bad about doing it. Then I felt incredibly bad about lying to my husband and I immediately repented to God for what I had done. Well the next thing that happened was just plain incredible...

I decided for some reason, to go to a bag of books and to pull out a book that I had not looked in for *several weeks*. The book had a bookmark marking the page where I had last read and this was some time ago. My natural instinct led me to open right where the bookmark had been left last. So I threw open the page bookmarked and the heading on that page was *"Lying to Others."* Immediate conviction hit me like a lightning bolt and I felt awful and sick about lying. So this was truly, truly amazing. You know I felt so bad about lying like that, that I asked the Lord for forgiveness right away and I knew I felt so terrible about it.

Numbers 32:23: *But if ye will not do so, behold, ye have sinned against the LORD: and be sure your sin will find you out.*

Do Not Let the Sun Go Down

One morning while traveling to school in our car—I spoke to Ethan about the importance of the verse in Ephesians that talks about not letting the sun go down on your anger. We talked a little about this verse and what it might mean—not staying angry after the sun goes down. I explained that God does not want us to get angry at each other and not settle it before the day is out so that the devil cannot use our anger to take control over us.

Right after dropping Ethan to his school that same morning—I continued to think about that verse. Then after checking my email messages, the same verse came up in my email devotions as the featured verse and lesson for the day. **Ephesians 4:26-27:** *Be ye angry, and sin not: let not the sun go down upon your wrath: Neither give place to the devil.* This was incredible—when you consider there are within the average Bible 1,281 plus pages. Yet, of all the many verses in the Bible this verse was my focused devotion after we spent our trip to school discussing this identical verse.

Dynamite

Truly one of the most incredible displays of the power of the Holy Spirit and signs and wonders in my life took place when my family and I were on a trip out of town. We were staying in a hotel room and I had decided to spend some time with the Lord by reading my Bible. I was reaching for the Bible and then, amazingly I threw open the Bible and to my terrific surprise my eyes fell on the word **"dynamite"** in the Bible. The word dynamite was used in the commentary about **Acts 1:8:** *But ye shall receive power, after that the Holy Ghost is come upon you: and ye shall be witnesses unto me both in Jerusalem, and in all Judaea, and in Samaria, and unto the uttermost part of the earth.* Holy Spirit power is like dynamite, and that is the word I turned to when I opened the Bible—DYNAMITE. When I flipped to this section and my eyes fell on the word *"DYNAMITE"* amazingly, the TV was on in our hotel room and the person on TV talking at the time said the word "DYNAMITE" at the exact time my eyes fell on the word "DYNAMITE."

As mentioned elsewhere, with an average Bible's number of words at 774,746, how in the world could I flip open the Bible, glance down and see the word **"dynamite"** and hear the word **"dynamite"** being said simultaneously as I read the same word? What are the odds of this happening? Talk about the power of the Holy Spirit! **Luke 1:37:** *For with God nothing shall be impossible.*

I can even remember a time that I was standing in my bathroom at home adjoining our bedroom. The TV in the bedroom was on and playing loudly in the background enough that I could hear it. As I was standing in front of the bathroom mirror, I was pondering the truth that "SURRENDER" was the answer to seeking God. Exactly after I thought the word "SURRENDER" in my mind, I heard someone on the TV playing in the background said the word "SURRENDER." It was like hearing an exact echo to my thought and it was remarkable.

Answering My Questions

Amazingly when I ask God questions, I have noticed that He many times answers my questions in creative ways within a day or so after I ponder the question. Here is a great example…One day I wondered about the incredible difference between Judas and Peter who were disciples of Jesus. One betrayed Christ to His enemies and then later killed himself in disgrace. The other, Peter denied Christ three times during the height of Jesus' struggle with His accusers. Peter, unlike Judas, was forgiven by Christ after His resurrection and Peter later became one of Jesus' greatest promoters. Now I talked to my Mother on the phone about this subject and pondered the diverse endings of the two disciples. Then later that evening I did the same thing, I spoke about this with my best friend and we both talked about the extreme variance between the outcomes of these two lives. I questioned how it was that Judas' life ended so differently from Peter's.

The next morning, my husband Steve asked me to drive him in the car to pick up something. Steve turned on the car radio and it is rare that I ever listen to the radio in the morning in the car when I am driving alone. However this morning, Steve turned on the radio and I heard two pastors involved in a discussion between them about the difference between Judas and Peter and how Judas ran away ultimately to his own demise and Peter was forgiven by Jesus. The pastors said the Bible speaks of how Satan entered into Judas. In addition, there were signs of Judas' ongoing corruption, which Peter did not share. I think it is just amazing the way I had thought of this question throughout the day prior and then to have two pastors on the radio discussing the similarities of the two disciples and the diverse ending between the two on a radio show the next morning. It was truly amazing.

Chapter Eight—Descend from Heaven

Descend from Heaven

A most incredible thing happened.

This event caused me to begin to realize that perhaps all the things I had been witnessing were much more than just wonderful coincidences (but truly God at work in my life). I had come to read a fascinating true story reported about a Jewish man in Jerusalem who was having the same dream repeatedly 19 times. He was so troubled that he asked many people what it might mean—but none of the Jewish Rabbis around him knew the meaning. One day some Christian ministers came through the area near this Jewish man's shop and he heard the Christian ministers together singing hymns he recognized from his reoccurring dreams. He summoned them over to his shop and asked them to hear about his repeating dream to see if they knew what the message was and explain it to him. The dream was straight out of **1 Thessalonians 4:16-17** and it was specifically about the rapture. The shopkeeper was asked if he knew who the "Conqueror" was in his dream. He did not know. The ministers explained that the man he saw was *Jesus* and they asked him if he wanted to become a Christian and he immediately chose to as well as his wife and his employees.

While I was reading this remarkable story, the TV was on in the room in the background and the movie about the life of the Apostle Paul was playing. I came to read the section of the story about the Jewish man, in which the ministers are reading this section of the Bible to him from **1 Thessalonians 4:16-17:** *For the Lord himself shall* **descend from heaven** *with a shout, with the voice of the archangel, and with the trump of God: and the dead in Christ shall rise first: Then we which are alive and remain shall be caught up together with them in the clouds, to meet the Lord in the air: and so shall we ever be with the Lord.*

Incredibly as I read these words in the story from the verse in **1 Thessalonians 4:16-17:** "DESCEND FROM HEAVEN"—I heard the actor in the movie about the Life of the Apostle Paul playing on TV *say the same words as I read with absolute synchronization.* I could not believe what just had happened. If I had tried to make this event happen—I am sure I could not have done it. I had no idea that when I read this particular phrase that the actor in the movie playing in the background would read the same phrase exactly when I read it—this was stunning to me. Surely, I could have written this off as a truly amazing coincidence only. But then this was just the beginning of an onslaught of similar events—so much so, that I had to admit that this just could not all be coincidences and I began to see it all for what it was—God's way of communicating to me just how he controls everything and knows everything I am doing along with everyone else. He is the Grand Weaver who brings together people and circumstances into our lives for reinforcement, communication, affirmations, reassurance, comfort, and teaching.

Now if you would like to read this true story about the Jewish shopkeeper's reoccurring dream about **1 Thessalonians 4:16-17** and his subsequent conversion to Christ you can find it in Christine Darg's new book, *"The Jesus Visions,"* in Chapter 4. The entire book is available online at www.jesusvisions.org/index.html.

Rain Cloud

One sunny day, I was standing outside by my car cleaning it out. While working on my car, I was playing a Christian song about being able to praise God in the storms of life. It was stored on the MP3 player I was listening to and when in the song, the lyrics about rain started playing, right then it started to rain. The rain came from a little cloud that had passed over me and it rained on the car I was working on too. Only it rained right where I was standing and no place else. *Remember, it was a perfectly sunny day.* Then the rain cloud passed over me for a few moments and then the rain stopped. Now this may have been extremely coincidental, but the music playing with lyrics about rain and a rain cloud showing up overhead to rain on me and only where I was standing and nowhere else.

My son came out by the car and said that the rain only came down where I was standing, and it was completely dry everywhere else except right where I was standing. The cloud moved on and it continued to be a sunny day without any further rain in sight. However, for this one brief moment, a rain cloud burst forth over me while the song played on about rain.

Job 37:11-16: *Also by watering he wearieth the thick cloud: he scattereth his bright cloud: And it is turned round about by his counsels: that they may do whatsoever he commandeth them upon the face of the world in the earth. He causeth it to come, whether for correction, or for his land, or for mercy. Hearken unto this, O Job: stand still, and consider the wondrous works of God. Dost thou know when God disposed them, and caused the light of his cloud to shine? Dost thou know the balancings of the clouds, the wondrous works of him which is perfect in knowledge?*

Still Small Voice
In the privacy of my bedroom, I was on the floor praying to God and something unexplainable came over me. I had a sudden powerful longing for Christ which came over me. I began to weep uncontrollably. I felt this incredibly sad feeling of wanting to be closer to Christ. The next thing that happened was quite unexpected and completely jolted me. I heard that still small voice—and He said to me as I wept, ***"Here I am."*** I was so startled I immediately quit crying and I knew it was the Lord speaking to me.

Isaiah 58:9: *Then shalt thou call, and the LORD shall answer; thou shalt cry, and he shall say, here I am.*

Living Water from the Well
Many times, I find that in the same day I will read a Bible verse from the Bible or my devotional study only to turn around and to read the identical verse or message through a different book I am reading on the same day. This happens to me so often and it is a wonderful confirmation to me for what I am studying. For example, I was reading on one morning a wonderful book called *"The Secret Place"* by Dr. Dale Fife who recounts through a vision of Christ how to obtain an intimate relationship with God and a section about ***drawing living water out of the well of God*** and that was what the whole section was about that I was reading.

I opened up the Bible *randomly* to **Isaiah 12:3**, and this is what I read next:

Isaiah 12:3: ***Therefore with joy shall ye draw water out of the wells of salvation.***

Ruby Ring
My husband, son, and I were waiting to for a table at a restaurant for dinner one evening. While we were waiting, I happened to look down at the ring on my finger. It must have belonged to my grandmother. I was fortunate to find it when I was clearing out my parent's house. Since my father has passed away and my mother says, it is not from her family I have no real way to know just whom the ring belonged to and how it was in my father's possession. It is in an extraordinary white gold antique setting probably from the 1920s, and it has two good-size red rubies. I wear it on my left hand and while waiting to be seated I was looking at this ring and thought to myself that it was nice I had gotten this family ring and that God had made that possible for me to have it. *I then next wondered what red rubies might mean to God?*

While pondering these things about the ring, we were taken to our table. Then while waiting for our food to come, I decided to read a little out of the book *"The Secret Place"* written by Dr. Dale Fife and it is about his personal visions of Christ. The book tells about obtaining an intimate relationship with Christ. Amazingly, the book talks about how God revealed to the writer in a vision that red rubies represent the blood of Christ.

I was stupefied the way I was thinking about this ruby ring I am wearing and what red rubies might mean to God—only to open this book up and have the next paragraph I read about a ruby ring. It was so strange and yet incredible. I did not know that this was going to be in this section of the book I was reading. I was stunned. At first, I thought this might just be an incredible coincidence. However, then I thought it was exceptionally odd that it would happen within minutes of each other and also the thought occurred to me that this sort of thing is happening to me frequently—every couple days... I will never think about my ring in the same way again.

Right Now!

While I was out grocery shopping—I had my MP3 player on and I was listening with my earphones to a taped broadcast of an interview with the author Shawn Bolz about his book titled "*Heaven's Economy.*" The interview I was listening to told about how to tap into God's resources for doing His work. I stepped into the store restroom and while I am listening to this taped interview, I hear the interviewer talking about tapping into God's resources and he says, "God wants you to do this ***RIGHT NOW!***" Just as I came into the restroom, I saw on the door right in front of me was a bunch of graffiti. All the graffiti had been blacked out with a marker except for just two words remaining and they were right in front of my face: ***"RIGHT NOW!"*** All the other words written before and after the "Right Now!" were completely blacked out. As I turned to hear the words "RIGHT NOW!" as they were said on the tape—I had turned to see the written words in front of my face, "RIGHT NOW!" *at the same exact moment.* Now I thought to myself, did the interviewer just say the words "Right Now" and am I seeing the words "Right Now" at the same time? Then, the interviewer spoke a second time and said, "I said that God wants you to do this ***Right Now!*** *a second time.* I almost fell over. I could not believe that this had happened.

Ethan's Holy Land Experience

Our family went to Orlando, Florida for a recent spring break vacation. While there, I really wanted to go to the Holy Land Experience, a theme park that depicts the life of Christ. It was great to see different parts of the park focusing on the life and times of Jesus. There was a kind of auditorium in the park in which the re-enactment of the Last Supper was performed.

Before the program started we were ushered into a room where we sitting in a row of chairs. While sitting there waiting for the show to begin, I looked up and on the ceiling around the top was written the different names of God. As I was sitting there waiting, I looked over and Ethan looked pale as if he had seen a ghost. He told me he just had a vision. We watched the program and waited until we were outside for him to tell me what happened.

Then Ethan told me that while we were waiting for the program to start, that something amazing happened to him. He said that he had suddenly left the room and went out into space and he was moving like the speed of light into space. But then, he described that he turned his head and then just as quickly he was back in the room again.

Ethan describes his experience in his own words this way:

We had gone to Florida for spring break to spend the week with my grandparents in their house they have down there. We had gone to the Holy Land Experience, which wasn't too far from where we were staying. After we were there for awhile, right after we saw the re-enactment of the Crucifixion we went to see the Last Supper play and right before the play had started I was taken out into outer space and I couldn't even see the sky. I was out in outer space and it was as if I was light, and stars were shooting by me like streams of light. Then next, I turned my head to look back and all of a sudden, I was back in the room. And while this was all going on I was sitting in this chair and all of a sudden I lost control of my body I slumped over and my spirit had left me and it was weird. And then all of a sudden I was back and I was slumped over and I was trying to figure out what just happened and then I leaned over to my mom to see if she had seen anything that had gone on and she said no and I told her all that had happened and she just looked at me and soon after that we left. At the time, it happened I felt peaceful but when I got back, it was shocking to me.

Chapter Nine—Wash Robes

Wash Robes

I was standing at my bathroom sink one day washing my hands and the Holy Spirit spoke to me saying,

"If you wash your hands frequently to rid yourself of germs and bacteria to keep from being physically ill, then why do you consider washing your robes less trivial?"

This was a stunning revelation to me. I knew it was the Holy Spirit because I have never in my life referred to seeking repentance from the Lord as washing robes—but that is what I learned after that when I looked up the phrase "washing robes." In the Bible the phrase can be found in the verse **Revelation 22:14.** You see, I was not accustom to saying the phrase "washing robes," but I admit I had heard of it used in the Bible before so I knew to look it up in the Bible and this is what I found:

Revelation 22:14: *Blessed are they that do his commandments, that they may have right to the tree of life, and may enter in through the gates into the city. (Other versions actually say, "Blessed are those who wash their robes.")*

If I expand on the lesson that I received from the Holy Spirit it would be that when **Revelation 22:14** states blessed are those who wash their robes—this is clearly not a future tense statement to someday wash robes in the future. It is not a past tense statement saying, "For one time only, blessed are those who have washed their robes." Plainly, the tense is present tense *wash their robes* and the Holy Spirit was making known to me that washing robes *or repentance* should be a frequent occurrence for the Christian. In fact, the frequency that He prescribed to me was as in washing hands to prevent disease, which we perform often.

So why would the act of "washing our robes" so frequently be needed? I believe that frequent repentance is necessary to enjoy a close communion with God, because *God is so very holy* and we are so very sinful. We need to repent regularly to stay close to God. Every time we approach God in prayer, we should first seek repentance through the precious blood of Christ. If we want to have our petitions heard and to partake in a close relationship with a holy God—then we need to be regularly repentant. This was the significant instruction I received from the Holy Spirit.

Christ has stepped in and provided His blood as a sufficient sacrifice to atone for our sins and to bridge the impossible gap between all of us evil men to a pure and Holy God. Nevertheless, as long as we are in these bodies and cursed by our sinful nature in this life then we must seek forgiveness and repentance and it is only with the blood of Christ given to us that we can be forgiven and able to approach God. God the Father then sees us through the covering of His Son Christ's blood. No one can enter to the Father in Heaven without first repenting and applying the blood of Christ to themselves and acknowledging Christ crucified.

As the Apostle Paul, so often stressed in his New Testament writings everything revolves around Christ crucified. The Bible points to Christ from beginning to end and without Christ crucified we are doomed. The act of God becoming man through His one and only son Jesus and dying for us was the only pure and perfect sacrifice to atone for our sins—past, present, future.

I consider this message to me from the Holy Spirit as a major gift. This gift was one of the reasons that I decided to write this book—so I could share the insight given to me with others. Through our admission of sin and acceptance of the blood of Christ, as the only means to our forgiveness, we can then come boldly to the throne of God and enjoy His fellowship. There is nothing we can do to *merit or earn* God's forgiveness—nothing. God's forgiveness given to us is an act of mercy—unmerited forgiveness. So then how can we successfully repent?

The way we repent successfully to God is to do it from a sincere, humble, broken heart, and acknowledging that only Christ has what we need for forgiveness. Repent means "to turn." When we turn by repenting, we should not turn back to our own evil ways—we should turn straight to Jesus for the only hope we have to enable us to turn from our sins and evil ways. We do not have what it takes to combat sin on our own. Jesus says *that apart from Him we are nothing.*

Our repentance should not be just another ritualistic act of works to impress God but rather an act of true remorse over our sinful condition and a humble admission that we desperately need Christ to turn away from evil. We need to wash our robes frequently to stay in close communion with a Holy God.

Psalms 24:3-4: *Who shall ascend into the hill of the LORD? Or who shall stand in his holy place?* **He that hath clean hands**, *and a pure heart; who hath not lifted up his soul unto vanity, nor sworn deceitfully.*

James 4:7-10: *Submit yourselves therefore to God. Resist the devil, and he will flee from you. Draw nigh to God, and he will draw nigh to you.* **Cleanse your hands**, *ye sinners; and purify your hearts, ye double minded. Be afflicted, and mourn, and weep: let your laughter be turned to mourning, and your joy to heaviness. Humble yourselves in the sight of the Lord, and he shall lift you up.*

Hebrews 10:22: *Let us draw near with a true heart in full assurance of faith, having our hearts sprinkled from an evil conscience, and our* **bodies washed with pure water.**

Isaiah 1:16: **Wash you, make you clean;** *put away the evil of your doings from before mine eyes; cease to do evil;*

Man Cannot Save Mankind

I once had this inner struggle of *how do you die to self?* One day I point-blank asked God, *"How does one die to oneself?"* Moreover, I admitted to Him that, "I don't quite understand this." Now you have to know that I was not really expecting an answer nor was I expecting to receive one even so quickly. Nevertheless, **immediately** the Holy Spirit flooded my mind with an answer. He gave me information instantaneously and this is the message that flooded into my mind: The message was that *man cannot be glorified because man cannot save mankind— whether it is celebrities, evangelists, CEOs, political leaders, or whoever, because ONLY JESUS can save mankind. So, by glorifying men it only leads us to destruction when we blindly follow the ideas, views, and ways of men.* When this happened I thought, "Wow, that is truly profound and I can understand that." It was so clear to me— man should not be glorified in any way, because men cannot lead men to true life. So that understanding, for me, made it easier to see the importance and significance of giving up "self."

We cannot save each other. **Acts 4:12** says: *Neither is there salvation in any other: for there is no other name under heaven given among men, whereby we*

We shall make a mistake if we make anyone our model save the Lord Jesus, for in another life but His there will be sure to be something in excess. I am sure it will be best for us, if we are Wesleyans, not always to try to do everything as John Wesley did it; and if we are Calvinists, much as we honor John Calvin, to remember that we shall go wrong if we try to season everything with the spirit of John Calvin. No man is fit to be a model for all men, except the Savior who redeemed men.

~Charles Spurgeon, Evangelist

must be saved. When we put other men up on pedestals because of their knowledge—whether they are well-known talk show hosts or political leaders and we follow after their teachings and ideas—we are not focusing our attention on the One who really deserves our adoration and admiration—Christ who alone can save mankind.

This is not a new problem—men have followed men to their eternal demise for centuries. Men have followed Adolf Hitler and his leadership. Men have followed scientists like Charles Darwin to disbelieve in intelligent design. Men have followed popular cult leaders like Jim Jones. How many times in the past and present, do men mistakenly follow other men and their philosophies that lead people away from Christ? Who alone can save mankind? This error is more prolific than ever because communication is more easily accessible to greater numbers of people than ever before. If our complete focus is not on Christ, then we are doomed. **John 14:6:** says: *Jesus saith unto him, I am the **way**, the **truth**, and the **life**: no man cometh unto the Father, but by me.*

We can more easily die to ourselves when we admit that we cannot save ourselves or anyone else. Our disease is a sinful "self" and the only cure is death to that "self" and life through Christ crucified.

Isaiah 31:1: *Woe to them that go down to Egypt for help; and stay on horses, and trust in chariots, because they are many; and in horsemen, because they are very strong; but they look not unto the Holy One of Israel, neither seek the LORD!*

Isaiah 45:21-22: *Tell ye, and bring them near; yea, let them take counsel together: who hath declared this from ancient time? Who hath told it from that time? Have not I the LORD? And there is no God else beside me; a just God and a Savior; there is none beside me. Look unto me, and be ye saved, all the ends of the earth: for I am God, and there is none else.*

Philippians 2:6-11: *Who, being in the form of God, thought it not robbery to be equal with God: But made himself of no reputation, and took upon him the form of a servant, and was made in the likeness of men: And being found in fashion as a man, he humbled himself, and became obedient unto death, even the death of the cross. Wherefore God also hath highly exalted him, and given him a name which is above every name: That at the name of Jesus every knee should bow, of things in heaven, and things in earth, and things under the earth; And that every tongue should confess that Jesus Christ is Lord, to the glory of God the Father.*

Jeremiah 17:5-8: *Thus saith the LORD; cursed be the man that trusteth in man, and maketh flesh his arm, and whose heart departeth from the LORD. For he shall be like the heath in the desert, and shall not see when good cometh; but shall inhabit the parched places in the wilderness, in a salt land and not inhabited. Blessed is the man that trusteth in the LORD, and whose hope the LORD is. For he shall be as a tree planted by the waters, and that spreadeth out her roots by the river, and shall not see when heat cometh, but her leaf shall be green; and shall not be careful in the year of drought, neither shall cease from yielding fruit.*

Chapter Ten—Be Holy

Be Holy

Leviticus 11:44: *For I am the LORD your God: ye shall therefore sanctify yourselves, and ye shall be holy; for I am holy: neither shall ye defile yourselves with any manner of creeping thing that creepeth upon the earth.*

Galatians 5:17-26:

For the flesh lusteth against the Spirit, and the Spirit against the flesh: and these are contrary the one to the other: so that ye cannot do the things that ye would. But if ye be led of the Spirit, ye are not under the law. Now the works of the flesh are manifest, which are these: Adultery, fornication, uncleanness, lasciviousness, Idolatry, witchcraft, hatred, variance, emulations, wrath, strife, seditions, heresies, Envyings, murders, drunkenness, revellings, and such like: of the which I tell you before, as I have also told you in the time past, that they which do such things shall not inherit the kingdom of God. But the fruit of the Spirit is love, joy, peace, longsuffering, gentleness, goodness, faith, Meekness, temperance: against such there is now law. And they that are Christ's have crucified the flesh with the affections and lusts. If we live in the Spirit let us also walk in the Spirit. Let us not be desirous of vain glory, provoking one another, envying one another.

The whole idea behind the verse **Leviticus 11:44** drove me crazy... I want you to know that I would plead with God in prayer over this verse about the problem with sin. Struggling about the idea of sin, I would say to God that I understood how *He could be holy*, but the idea of walking away from sinfulness seemed to be the most impossible concept. To give you an example of my stress over this subject, I would read several books and meet with my church pastor occasionally to discuss this issue and still be so perplexed. Was God "for real" when He said for us to be holy?

So I pled with God in prayer many times saying that I thought the idea of being holy was definitely a good one, but I just did not see how the average person could conquer this one. However, I did often pray reminding God that whoever hungered and thirsted after righteousness would be filled. I knew that truth was in the Bible although I still did not comprehend it. **Matthew 5:6:** *Blessed are they which do hunger and thirst after righteousness: for they shall be filled.*

One day, God gave me an earth-shattering "light bulb" moment after a lot of frustrating contemplation about this subject.

It dawned on me that God is Holy and pure 100 percent of the time...just like the needle on a compass, that always points North. If you are lost in a woods and you have a compass with a reliable needle that always points to the North, you can find your way out of the forest. God is like that reliable compass needle that points North without fail. It also occurred to me that in hell, there would be nobody or nowhere to turn for complete truth. There will be no truth in hell, no compass that always points North. There is less and less truth found in even this world today.

At that moment, I grasped that you cannot pursue that which you do not cherish. Then I realized what a limited commodity truth, justice, righteousness, purity, and holiness is in this life and completely void in hell. Suddenly I had this intense emotion about how significant God's holiness is and how important it is that He has always been and is always consistently pure and holy. This truth hit me so intensely between my eyes that for days I would weep when I thought about how much I truly valued and cherished God's righteousness and holiness.

God has never been anything at anytime but perfect, pure, just, righteous, good, sinless, and holy. He always will be holy and you can count on it. What else anywhere can you ever count on but that? Where can you ever turn to find one who represents absolute justice, absolute truth, absolute purity, and absolute holiness except for God?

Bibles

During a recent spring break, we made a trip down to Orlando, Florida. I took some Bibles with us to give away to whomever and whenever the Spirit moved. Now we were visiting at St. Petersburg beach and I was sitting in a picnic shelter while my son Ethan played on the beach. A man came up to feed some birds and he was very friendly and spoke to me. I talked to him a little bit and I was not even reading a Bible at the time. He told me he came to that area after work to feed the birds.

We were just conversing and making small talk, then amazingly he said to me that he was attending a Bible study, but he did not own his own Bible. I could not believe that he would say this to me out of the blue. So next, I told him to wait a minute and I then ran to our car and grabbed one of the Bibles I had brought along on our trip. When I returned with a Bible to give him, he looked surprised. He showed me the business card of his Bible study leader and he was some sort of minister, so I knew he was telling the truth about his Bible study. I still cannot get over how this man just informed me that he needed a Bible—a stranger who I could give a free Bible. You know if you make yourself available, God will use you, sometimes in unique ways.

Three Bathrooms

Now I must have been born with a rare bladder disorder. My parents first detected this problem when I was only in second grade. This rare disorder means that my bladder is dysfunctional and basically I am handicapped. I am used to it, but it seems to be more of a nuisance to my family—especially on family trips in the car.

Over the years, I have never really ever bothered God with my frustration over this problem. Then that one day came and I asked Him outright why He had not chosen to heal me of this problem. As quickly as I asked the question—an answer came at that next moment to me from the Lord and He said to me audibly, *"I gave you a house with three bathrooms."* I was stupefied by the answer I received and with the swiftness it was delivered. Yes, I was humbled once again. We must learn to praise God no matter what our circumstances.

This was one of my most humbling moments. I had many times complained about the house we had moved to for various reasons. When we moved in, it had many things wrong with it. I can remember being quite annoyed with this house and never thinking about how God gives us everything that we have. So much of the time, we seem to be oblivious to this truth as if we are in charge of our lives apart from God. This was deeply troubling to me and I began to see my overall ungratefulness to God. I felt shameful at all the times I took my circumstances for granted and the little credit I had given to God for what I possessed. I had nothing to do with anything I owned really. It all has come from His great hand—everything we have and own comes from God.

My emotions ran the gamut. I *was* excited to hear from God and so quickly. This was not even anything I expected to have happen when I asked the question. I was thrilled to realize that He did indeed care about my personal physical plight. When you read about how much God cares for us in the Bible it is one thing—but to hear it directly from Him is also humbling. All at once, I wanted to crawl under a rock because I had been such a spoiled child complaining about my personal circumstances. You talk about humiliation, with one blow I was brought down several notches back to earth. How could I have not seen that everything I owned was directly from the Lord and I should be appreciative for all that I have and never ungrateful. What a truly humbling moment and I felt badly that the Holy Spirit had to do this to wake me up but glad that I saw things from a fresh perspective. In addition, I know that God chooses where we all are to live as described in **Acts 17:26**.

Acts 17:26: *And hath made of one blood all nations of men for to dwell on all the face of the earth, and hath determined the times before appointed, and the bounds of their habitation*

Matthew 10:42

While at one of my son's baseball games, one of his fellow players ran over to his parents because he was sick and throwing up. After a couple minutes, I went over to the child's mom and offered to get some water for him. She did not hesitate to say, "Yes" to my offer for water. So, I ran over to my son and told him I needed his unopened cold water bottle. He gave me his water, so I could give to the sick baseball player. After purchasing a new bottle for my son, we had to leave the game early to go to another activity. While we were riding in the car, I turned on the CD player and my son's Bible story CD was playing and the narrator on his CD immediately proceeded to read a Bible verse. Here is that verse:

Matthew 10:42: *And whosoever shall give to drink unto one of these little ones a cup of cold water only in the name of a disciple, verily I say unto you, he shall in no wise lose his reward.*

Walking on My Dad's Feet

My Father has been gone about 14 years now and I had recently spoken to God about missing my earthly Father. I reminisced with God about the way my Father would let me walk on his feet in a sort of dancing movement when I was just a young child and I suggested that someday we should also do this when we meet. The very, next day to my great surprise, my son walked up to me and began to walk on my feet in a dance movement. *He has never done this before.* I wondered what prompted him to do such a thing and he only said that he had no explanation and he just did it. This was to me an awesome sign from God that He indeed was hearing my conversations with Him.

Chapter Eleven—Spiritual Milestones

Spiritual Milestones

Luke 19:39-40: *And some of the Pharisees from among the multitude said unto him, Master, rebuke thy disciple. And he answered and said unto them, I tell you that, if these should hold their peace, the stones would immediately cry out.*

You could say that I have been wondering if many of the unusual occurrences that I have been experiencing were real or just some extremely amazing coincidences of some kind. Over time, I have gone back and forth over some of these in my mind, trying to discern if perhaps I have been reading too much into these incidences. I sure wanted to believe in them—but I did not want to believe in something that was not real. Then something amazing happened to completely dispel and blow my theory out of the water that what I had been experiencing was just a bunch of incredible coincidences.

My husband, son, and I were traveling along a rural country road in the car, while not far from our family cabin, and Steve had music playing as I strained to hear the lyrics. I heard in the music playing the words: *Jesus is the Rock*. I repeated the words in my mind in confirmation of the lyrics I had just heard: "Yes, Jesus is the Rock." At the very moment that I said the word "Rock" in my mind, I looked out the window of the car and saw the sign on a *very* rural road that read "Rock Church." And, while thinking the word "Rock"—I simultaneously read the word "Rock." Immediately I thought this was very odd—in fact, what are the odds that this should happen—we were on an extremely remote rural country road with a very limited number of signs of any kind. However, this isn't the end of what happened…

I had been thinking about all these wonderful experiences I have been having with God and to me they are precious jewels. And, then it occurred to me that I wanted to create something to remember and cherish all these special moments. I decided to do something to commemorate these things and just for fun, I went to the store to purchase gold spray paint. That evening, even though it had become dark, I was determined to start my craft project. We were at our family cabin and I got our flashlight and started to search for rocks outside the cabin. My plan was to spray paint the rocks with gold paint and then to create a kind of physical remembrance of my cherished moments with God.

After spray painting several rocks in gold and writing a few things about my special memories on these "commemorative" rocks, I decided to retire to the book I was reading at the time titled *"The Hidden Kingdom (Journey Into the Heart of God)"* by Dr. Dale Fife, who wrote to share the visions He had received from God. As I was reading his book, I began thinking to myself and jokingly I began to wonder what I would think if there would be something I would come to in the book written about rocks…

…The next section I turned to read in the book (with no foreknowledge of what I was about to read), was titled: "Spiritual Stones"—and the premise of this section shows the author having a revealing vision of God and His ways. I was flabbergasted that I should be collecting stones right before reading about stones. *The spiritual stones the author wrote about were about the spiritual milestones—stepping stones—in a person's life leading to the Kingdom of God. My spray-painted stones were to be used to mark spiritual milestones and to commemorate special moments with God in my life—the similarity between the two meanings was uncanny.* And, then remember how earlier in this very same day, I had heard music lyrics about Jesus being the "Rock" and I had thought about Jesus being the "Rock" at the very same time I see the word "Rock" on a sign on a very remote country road? Well in the same section about Spiritual Stones that I was reading, the verse came up from **1 Corinthians 10:4** which read: *And did all drink the same spiritual drink: for they drank of that spiritual Rock that followed them: and that Rock was Christ.*

The author goes on to state that the Spiritual Stones were cut from the Rock of the Lord himself. The entire section speaks of "*Spiritual Stones*" and "*Christ as the Rock.*" I had absolutely no foreknowledge that I might be reading these things in this book. This section of the book speaks of the requirements of reaching the narrow road to Heaven—this has been a prayer that I have prayed on many occasions. Many times I had prayed to God that if the road to Heaven was a narrow one and many did not find it—then Lord, please get me to that road.

I really felt that this book was meant for me to read and to understand…and there was no questioning or denying what had just happened to me that day. I was so overcome by this event—I could hardly sleep that night. I knew then for sure that none of the other things that had happened to me was simply mere coincidences.

Then, I went to the Internet and was amazed to discover further information and to find out that God's people often use _memorial stones_ to commemorate special milestones in their walk with God. This truly amazed me—given that I had decided to pursue this without any idea at all that God's people did this and to be shown in the same night that this was the case through the book I was reading was absolutely incredible. I have no explanation for it—except that it was given to me by God. I promise you when I created my personal _memorial stones_ dedicated to all my "high points" with God. I did not know anything previously about memorial stones. I just thought it was a fun idea at the time and I had no idea about the historic significance of such an event beforehand.

Here is what I later discovered was in the Bible:

Exodus 28:9-12: *And thou shalt take two onyx stones, and engrave on them the names of the children of Israel: Six of their names on one stone, and the other six names of the rest on the other stone, according to their birth. With the work of an engraver in stone, like the engravings of a signet, shalt thou engrave the two stones with the names of the children of Israel: thou shalt make them to be set in pouches of gold. And thou shalt put the two stones upon the shoulders of the ephod for **stones of memorial** unto the children of Israel: and Aaron shall bear their names before the LORD upon his two shoulders for a memorial.*

Exodus 39:6-7: *And they wrought onyx stones enclosed in pouches of gold, graven, as signets are graven, with the names of the children of Israel. And he put them on the shoulders of the ephod, that they should be **stones for a memorial** to the children of Israel; as the LORD commanded Moses.*

Joshua 4:1-9: *And it came to pass, when all the people were clean passed over Jordan, that the LORD spake unto Joshua, saying, Take you twelve men out of the people, out of every tribe a man, And command ye them, saying, Take you hence out of the midst of Jordan, out of the place where the priests' feet stood firm, twelve stones, and ye shall carry them over with you, and leave them in the lodging place, where ye shall lodge this night. Then Joshua called the twelve men, whom he had prepared of the children of Israel, out of every tribe a man: And Joshua said unto them, Pass over before the ark of the LORD your God into the midst of Jordan, and take you up every man of you a stone upon his shoulder, according unto the number of the tribes of the children of Israel: That this may be a sign among you, that when your children ask their fathers in time to come, saying, What mean ye by these stones? Then ye shall answer them, That the waters of Jordan were cut off before the ark of the covenant of the LORD; when it passed over Jordan, the waters of Jordan were cut off: and **these stones shall be for a memorial unto the children of Israel for ever**. And the children of Israel did so as Joshua commanded, and took up twelve stones out of the midst of Jordan, as the LORD spake unto Joshua, according to the number of the tribes of the children of Israel, and carried them over with them unto the place where they lodged, and laid them down there. And Joshua set up twelve stones in the midst of Jordan, in the place where the feet of the priests which bare the ark of the covenant stood: and they are there unto this day.*

Genesis 31:43-54: *And Laban answered and said unto Jacob, These daughters are my daughters, and these children are my children, and these cattle are my cattle, and all that thou seest is mine: and what can I do this day unto these my daughters, or unto their children which they have born? Now therefore come thou, let us make a covenant, I and thou; and let it be for a witness between me and thee. And Jacob took a stone, and set it up for a pillar. And Jacob said unto his brethren, Gather stones; and they took stones, and made an heap: and they did eat there upon the heap. And Laban called it Jegarsahadutha: but Jacob called it Galeed. And Laban said, This heap is a witness between me and thee this day. Therefore was the name of it called Galeed; And Mizpah; for he said, The LORD watch between me and thee, when we are absent one from another. If thou shalt afflict my daughters, or if thou shalt take other wives beside my daughters, no man is with us; see, God is witness betwixt me and thee. And Laban said to Jacob, Behold this heap, and behold this pillar, which I have cast betwixt me and thee: This heap be witness, and this pillar be witness, that I will not pass over this heap to thee, and that thou shalt not pass over this heap and this pillar unto me, for harm. The God of Abraham, and the God of Nahor, the God of their father, judge betwixt us. And Jacob sware by the fear of his father Isaac. Then Jacob offered sacrifice upon the mount, and called his brethren to eat bread: and they did eat bread, and tarried all night in the mount.*

Genesis 35:14: *And Jacob set up a pillar in the place where he talked with him, even a pillar of stone: and he poured a drink offering thereon, and he poured oil thereon.*

Why not create your own pillar of memorial stones commemorating special milestones in your journey/walk with God? What are some of the highlights in your life that have brought you closer to the Lord? Dedicate a stone to memorialize and remember each event.

God and Beds

My son Ethan and I had to run out for a late lunch at a nearby restaurant and the waitress we had was friendly. She told us she had a son Ethan's age. I asked her how many kids she had and she said four. I said, "Wow how do you do it?" "The Lord," was her immediate reply. And I agreed, "Yeah that is how I do it too."

She started to tell me that she had just moved from Georgia and that her husband had really hurt her physically and she had to get out with her kids. She said she had been recovering from cancer as well. She said her grandmother and uncle recently passed away and that was the last family she knew in the area. I asked her, "So you are a single parent?" I enquired if she had found a church to go to and she replied, "No, but I am looking for one." I suggested that she come to my church and I told her about my church. She said she might want to come to my church. Then I asked her if she needed anything and she said she needed beds because she and her four children were sleeping on a full bed together or on blankets on the floor because they only had one bed among them. I told her I was sure we could help her. I took her name and phone number. She said they also had nothing—they came to the area with nothing.

That very same afternoon I kept thinking—I need beds—where can I get beds? I thought to myself new beds are expensive and used bed mattresses are sometimes not so good and she has four kids.

I went to a juvenile center ministry meeting that night and afterwards I decided to take a long way home and I was talking to God in the car about this situation with needing the beds. A friend of mine's son had gone to church camp with my son the year before and I wanted to find out if he wanted to go to camp again. Their phone number had changed and I did not have the new number. So, I decided to stop by their house while I was near it.

I stopped by my friend's house and she came to the door and we talked a little about camp, and then she said the most extraordinary thing: *she asked me if I needed beds?* Surprised I said, "What?" She repeated, *"Do you need any beds?"* I replied, "Are you kidding?" She answered, "No I have a bunch of beds I want to get rid of."

So, I told my friend about the lady I met earlier that same day and her needs. She and her mom, who was also there, were amazed. She told me that she had a bunk bed with a full-size mattress on the bottom and a twin mattress on top. The second bed she had gotten brand new from someone was a twin bunk bed. I offered to pay her for the beds, but she said she wanted them to go to someone who really needed them. There were exactly enough beds for four kids. Soon after our conversation, I hopped in my car—pretty stunned—and drove back to the restaurant where I met this woman. She saw me come into the restaurant and she remembered me. I told her I had beds for her and told her the story as she was so amazed and we agreed that this was a miracle from God. She said she was really relying on God to carry her.

I was so stunned by this event, that around 3:30 p.m. this women I have never met before tells me she desperately needs beds. I then visited a friend randomly by 8 p.m. who has beds to give away on the same day and there are enough beds for four kids—exactly what they needed.

The next day, I visited my church's sister church which is in the same area the woman lives—the inner city. I spoke with the interim pastor who says these hardship stories are commonplace in the area. Some people had advised me not to get too involved or too close to this situation and I mentioned it to this inner city church pastor. He responded by taking me aside, and he said he had a Bible verse he wanted to give me. He told me to remember **Galatians 6:9** and he quoted it with great ease to me—as if it was a verse, he knew well:

Galatians 6:9: *And let us not be weary in well doing: for in due season we shall reap, if we faint not.*

I did make a note of the verse he gave me, but I was not prepared for what happened to me that same day. So, I came home later and I decided to check my email along with my daily devotional email. To my amazement, I received an email that was all about the single Bible verse **Galatians 6:9**! It was the same verse the inner city church pastor had impressed on me to remember, that same day. Of course, this was an amazing confirmation from the Lord to continue to help this needy family. Once you make a commitment for the Lord to give Him your life, I believe whole-heartedly that if you desire to help others, God will provide you with opportunities and give you the needed resources to make a difference.

Chapter Twelve—The Whirlwind*

The Whirlwind*

Acts 2:1-2: *And when the day of Pentecost was fully come, they were all with one accord in one place. And suddenly there came a sound from heaven as of a rushing mighty wind and it filled the entire house where they were sitting.*

During a recent summer while staying at our family cabin, Pentecost weekend in 2007, my son Ethan, age ten at that time, came to me pretty shaken up. He said he thought he'd had a dream—but he also said he was awake—this happened in the morning. Now, he told me that in this vision, he is standing outside and up in the sky is a dot and he looks up and as the dot gets closer and closer to him, it becomes larger. As it grows closer to him, he cries out to God and then he briefly sees people going up into the sky all around him and then it ends. He said there were many people going up into the sky around him.

Now I see that what he is telling me has him shook up and he is not one to ever describe such an event. So at this point, I just went about fixing breakfast and soon I realized that he has his paint sets out and he is trying to draw a picture of what he had seen. He has never done anything like this before. Next, I am thinking to myself, "Wow, maybe there is more to this than I think perhaps..."

What he draws is a circular object in black and light lavender colors. He says the lavender represents light and in the center, it looks like "energy" or "streaks of electricity," and it was not the usual picture that a 10-year-old would draw. Next, he explains to me that he saw a whirlwind not a tornado in his vision. I am thinking that this is all a strange thing for a kid to say.

Later that day, I am trying to think all this through and I decided to go to my Bible and see if I can find any pertinent information. As I mentioned before, it was Pentecost weekend when this event happened. I opened my Bible up randomly and I looked down. I first glanced in the Book of Acts at a reference to the historic Pentecost in verse **Acts 2:1:** *And when the day of Pentecost was fully come, they were all with one accord in one place.*

In addition, I thought that this was odd to open to this because it was precisely Pentecost weekend. Next, I glanced to the other page and my eyes immediately fell on the words: **your sons and daughters will prophesy** from the verse **Acts 2:17:** *And it shall come to pass in the last days, saith God, I will pour out of my Spirit upon all flesh: and your sons and your daughters shall prophesy, and your young men shall see visions, and your old men shall dream dreams.*

I was amazed that I should randomly first open to a reference about Pentecost on Pentecost weekend and then next see the verse about sons prophesying. This seemed incredible to me, but we became busy with other things and I did not speak of his vision too much again for a little while.

About three weeks later, a woman I had described Ethan's vision to, contacted me again and told me that she had read somewhere that someone else had a reported a vision of a whirlwind recently and that maybe I would want to check it out. I did check it out and I was amazed to learn through someone else's vision that God takes the form of a whirlwind. I was not aware that God is in the whirlwind and so I looked up several verses one day to learn more about this truth. Here is what I then discovered in the Bible:

Nahum 1:3: *The LORD is slow to anger, and great in power, and will not at all acquit the wicked:* **the LORD hath his way in the whirlwind** *and in the storm, and the clouds are the dust of his feet.*

Jeremiah 23:19: *Behold,* **a whirlwind of the LORD is gone forth in fury,** *even a grievous whirlwind: it shall fall grievously upon the head of the wicked.*

Jeremiah 4:13: *Behold, he shall come up as clouds,* **and his chariots shall be as a whirlwind:** *his horses are swifter than eagles. Woe unto us! For we are spoiled.*

2 Kings 2:1: *And it came to pass,* **when the LORD would take up Elijah into heaven by a whirlwind** *that Elijah went with Elisha from Gilgal.*

2 Kings 2:11: *And it came to pass, as they still went on, and talked, that, behold, there appeared a chariot of fire, and horses of fire, and parted them both asunder;* **and Elijah went up by a whirlwind into heaven.**

Immediately after looking up these verses, I realized that frequently God is referred to as in the whirlwind. While I was home alone, I had decided to pray about this. For some reason, I decided to retrieve my Bible and to read it aloud during my prayer. Without any preplanning or thought, I opened the Bible randomly to Psalms and I began reading there aloud in the midst of my praying. With no foreknowledge of what I turned to read, I came to a verse about God as in a whirlwind. This happened immediately after looking up several verses about God being in the whirlwind before I prayed. I was shocked that this happened.

After my discoveries of finding out that God was referred to as in a "Whirlwind" in the Bible, I wanted to go back to Ethan and talk with him further about his whirlwind vision. I talked to him again about this vision and reconfirmed that it had happened and that he saw something like a black hole with lightning, energy, and light. I was further awed when I questioned him about the statement he made to me right after he had this experience. He said to me the morning of his vision, "Mom it was a whirlwind, not a tornado." So I asked him did he know what a whirlwind was and how did he know the difference between a whirlwind and a tornado which he told me right after he had this vision. He stated then that he did not even know what a whirlwind was nor did he know the difference between a tornado and a whirlwind. I even went online after that and showed him what a whirlwind looked like and how it differed from a tornado. He really did not know these things.

I believe that God gave him the words that day that it was a whirlwind and not a tornado that he had seen. Ethan and I went online and looked up whirlwind pictures so that he could know about whirlwinds. So prior to this vision experience, Ethan did not know about whirlwinds and the difference between a whirlwind and a tornado at all.

It is fascinating to note that Ethan's hand-painted picture he made of what he witnessed was not the view of a whirlwind that most people would likely think of drawing. Most people would probably draw a whirlwind as a long slender column reaching into the sky with a view from the side of it. Ethan's rendering of what he saw was amazingly a circular image with energy or lightning streaks inside the circle. It was as if the whirlwind had been drawn from the perspective of being straight under it and looking up inside it from below.

Ezekiel 1:1-8: *Now it came to pass in the thirtieth year, in the fourth month, in the fifth day of the month, as I was among the captives by the river of Chebar,* **that the heavens were opened, and I saw visions of God.** *In the fifth day of the month, which was the fifth year of king Jehoiachin's captivity, The word of the LORD came expressly unto Ezekiel the priest, the son of Buzi, in the land of the Chaldeans by the river Chebar; and the hand of the LORD was there upon him. And* **I looked, and, behold, a whirlwind came out of the north,** *a great cloud, and a fire infolding itself, and a brightness was about it, and out of the midst thereof as the color of amber, out of the midst of the fire. Also out of the midst thereof came the likeness of four living creatures. And this was their appearance; they had the likeness of a man. And every one had four faces, and every one had four wings. And their feet were straight feet; and the sole of their feet was like the sole of a calf's foot: and they sparkled like the color of burnished brass. And they had the hands of a man under their wings on their four sides; and they four had their faces and their wings.*

Now if someone actually were to report seeing a real-life whirlwind, most likely they would draw it from the perspective of standing beside it as if looking at it as a column-shaped windstorm. What person ever depicts a whirlwind they have actually seen from the position of being exactly under it and looking up inside it—unless of course you were like Elijah, who in the Bible was taken to heaven up inside the whirlwind? Ethan said of the whirlwind overhead that it was the circumference of a van all around him in his vision. In addition, I think it is interesting to note that Ethan had drawn energy or lightning within the center of his picture of the whirlwind. This was another detail I noticed that was in **Ezekiel 1:1-8**. He would not have known this information before hand.

At the close of Ethan's vision, he describes seeing people all around him going up into the sky. I believe that the vision he was having was of the rapture of God's people to Himself.

Here is Ethan's version of what happened to him that morning in his own words:
I was on a camping trip to our family cabin with a friend and I had said a prayer to God asking that He would talk to me and He did. He gave me a vision of a whirlwind all of a sudden I was transported to a rocky beach and I was standing on a rock and I saw this speck in the sky and it got bigger and bigger until it looked like a tunnel it came over me and I was sucked up and I briefly saw like flashes of light streaming up around me they looked like transparent pieces of light and they were all over me—all around me were people that were like lights and like spirits they were going up all around me. It all felt timeless. The whirlwind around me was like a giant tunnel going on and on up into the sky and it was large around me.

And then I came back and my friend who spent the night was sprawled all over me. Immediately I got up and went downstairs because we were spending the night in the loft of our cabin. I immediately told my mom about what I had seen and how I said it was from God. I then got my paint set and drew a picture of the whirlwind.

*You can see Ethan's drawing of the whirlwind he saw on the cover of this book.

The Prayer Chapel
Whenever I stay at our family cabin at our church campground, I am always looking for a place where I can be to myself alone to pray. Many occasions I have seen the campground prayer chapel closed up and I stop to see if it is open. One time, I tried the door and as always, it was locked and I decided to talk to the campground caretaker to ask him about it. I asked him why the chapel was always closed. He said that it had been closed for a very long time and had even been used for storing things at one time. I asked him if I could use it for prayer and he said it was pretty bad inside. I asked him if I could clean it out—and he said, "Well if you want to," and he offered to open it up and show me inside.

It was just as he said all dirty, dusty, and full of spider webs. I was bitten badly in the first five minutes I was in there, probably by spiders. Still, I was excited about the little chapel being cleaned and opened. Others pitched in, my son and husband helped with clean up. Our caretaker cleared out the bushes around the chapel and his wife fixed up the landscaping in the front. She also cleared off all the poison ivy vines all over the back of the chapel (even though she was highly allergic to poison ivy).

The chapel is about the size of a single car garage with a lovely high vaulting ceiling and five little stained glass windows, four on the sides and one in the back. There was a beautiful portrait of Jesus up on the wall with the light shining on Him. It was the height of sadness to see this Holy space full of bugs and Jesus' picture covered with spider webs.

Over the front of the chapel was a glass block cross, which had been lit many years before. My husband, son, and I went to the store to look for special lights to light up the glass block cross. We found the perfect lighting for it, but it was cost-prohibitive for us to buy so we left the store dejected and without lighting. Still we had many people at church camp coming by the chapel to see it open for the first time in many, many years. Inside the chapel there was a memorial to church pastors, who had passed away, updated to 1989.

The next day, I was strolling along the road in front of the chapel during our family camp week, a woman came up next to me, and I happened to speak to her. She said she had heard the chapel was open and she wanted to see inside it because she had come from Chicago for one evening only to be at the memorial service and she was on her way back to Chicago. Her parents were both church pastors and had recently since passed away. I told her I would take her in to see the chapel and we talked about it and she seemed so happy to see it open again.

As we were walking out, she looked up at the unlit cross and asked if the light worked. I told her, "No" and that we could not afford the light fixtures right then to fix it. She asked me what we needed to fix it financially and I told her. She said to me, "Done." With that word, she turned to write a check and for the exact amount that we needed to fix the light and told us to get it lit up. I was shocked that I had just met this woman who was only coming to camp for a brief time, and that I should run into her and she would provide me with the exact amount of money needed to fix the light. Only recently, we did not have the money needed to repair the chapel light. It was so much like God saying, "Not good enough—this is my Holy space and I want the cross lit and here are the resources to do it." Needless to say, right after that we got the cross lit up like a beacon and it is beautiful.

Do you remember when Jesus went into the Temple of God and he drove out the moneychangers and told them to stop turning His Father's house into a marketplace? The Bible says, in verse **John 2:17:** *And his disciples remembered that it was written, the zeal of thine house hath eaten me up.*

My Closet

Steve and I were abruptly awakened from sleep one night. Our bedroom closet center-brace ripped out of the wall and the clothing rod fell to the ground. We discovered that the center brace, holding up the closet rod and the shelf above, was not attached to a wood wall beam. The rod was just attached to the dry wall and this caused the clothing rod to give way. The rod with the clothes came down and all my clothes were on the floor of the closet by the next day.

The next morning, I began to pick up all my clothes and fold them and put the hangers in piles in the bedroom. Ethan was home for the summer from school and he was around to help me sort the hangers. The TV was playing, but for some reason I decided to change the channel from what was on TV and turn to Joyce Meyers Ministry. She is funny and interesting, so I had decided to watch her TV show instead.

Right after changing the channel to Joyce Meyers, the top shelf in my closet, which was barely hanging on, fell down. Down came all of the stuff on the shelf tumbling to the floor. At the exact moment after the shelf fell to the ground, Joyce Meyers on TV said, *"You are cleaning out your closet and all your things are falling to the floor."* Then she goes on to talk about her message. My son and I looked at each other with complete shock.

The Dove

As I was driving down a neighborhood street on my way to meet Ethan and Steve for dinner, I looked up into the blue sky and I saw cloud formation that identically resembled a dove. I did not have a camera or I would have taken a picture. This cloud had a tail, wing, body, head, beak, and looked to me exactly like a dove. I did not think that it looked like a robin, hummingbird, or eagle. I thought it was exactly like a dove. Now as I continued to stare up at this unique cloud formation mesmerized by its perfect form of a dove. Later on after seeing this amazing perfectly shaped "dove" cloud in the sky, I went to my Bible and I discovered this interesting verse in the Bible with a reference to both a dove and clouds in Isaiah:

Isaiah 60:8: *Who are these that fly as a cloud and as the doves to their windows?*

The next day, while I was waiting for my car to be serviced, I decided check out the Internet while in the waiting room. I looked up information on this particular verse **Isaiah 60:8**. I was very interested in what this particular verse from the Bible might mean. At the same moment, the TV in the waiting room was also playing in the background. As I was reading online about the meaning of this particular verse and as I came to the word "DOVE," at the exact same moment, someone on TV said the word "DOVE" just as I read the word "DOVE" online with absolute precision. At the time, I thought what could be the chances of such a thing happening? However, this sort of thing was happening to me all the time.

Job 37:15: *Dost thou know when God disposed them, and caused the light of his cloud to shine?*

Psalms 135:7: *He causeth the vapors to ascend from the ends of the earth; he maketh lightnings for the rain; he bringeth the wind out of his treasuries.*

Psalms 147:8: *Who covereth the heaven with clouds, who prepareth rain for the earth, who maketh grass to grow upon the mountains.*

Door off the Hinges

One night about 3:00 a.m., I woke from my sleep and as I was sitting up in my bed, I heard very clearly the Lord speaking to me and He said simply a phrase familiar from the Bible,

"Behold, I stand at the door and knock."

Here is the complete verse from the Bible: **Revelation 3:20:** *Behold, I stand at the door, and knock: if any man hear my voice, and open the door, I will come in to him, and will sup with him, and he with me.*

The next phrase after "Behold, I stand at the door and knock" is the phrase, "if anyone hears my voice and opens the door." This is interesting to me since I heard His voice say the words, "Behold I stand at the door and knock." This particular verse comes from the letter in Revelation written to the Laodician church—the church that was neither hot nor cold. This particular phrase in the Bible refers to Christ's request to the individual to come to Jesus for communion and fellowship with Him. The only way to assure communion with Christ is through sincere repentance of our sins, to which Jesus is faithful to forgive and to embrace the person who desires a close relationship with Him.

Another time I was recalling the experience of hearing at 3:00 a.m. the words spoken by the Lord, "Behold I stand at the door and knock." That day I told the Lord, in a very joking way—that not only did I want to open the door for Him *that I was taking the door off its hinges!* Then a couple hours later that day I had made this wild declaration to God about *taking the door off its hinges,* my son happened to be watching a cartoon video on TV. I looked up, and the cartoon *character is standing in front of a door and suddenly he takes the door off its hinges.* I was stunned, because just a bit earlier I had been joking with God to forget about me opening the door for Him, because I was taking it off its hinges!

I was at my mother's place and my son was watching his video cartoon while she and I carried on a conversation. I was trying to describe to my Mom about collecting the spiritual stones (that I wrote about previously) and suddenly my son and mother start laughing. I turned around to see the cartoon character being chased by a large rock that was breaking up into a bunch of little stones. Everyone watching thinks it is so funny that in the cartoon there is a bunch of stones running away. This happens exactly while I am trying to talk to them about stones. I want you to know that I believe that the Lord has a terrific sense of humor.

Hebrews 11:6: *But without faith it is impossible to please him: for he that cometh to God must believe that he is, and that he is a rewarder of them that diligently seek him.*

Revelation 3:20-22: *Behold, I stand at the door, and knock: if any man hear my voice, and open the door, I will come in to him, and will sup with him, and he with me. To him that overcometh will I grant to sit with me in my throne, even as I also overcame, and am set down with my Father in his throne. He that hath an ear, let him hear what the Spirit saith unto the churches.*

Luke 12:35-36: *Let your loins be girded about, and your lights burning; And ye yourselves like unto men that wait for their lord, when he will return from the wedding; that when he cometh and knocketh, they may open unto him immediately.*

Dear Reader, Christ stands at your door and knocks. Invite Him into your life as your Savior, Redeemer, Counselor, Rescuer, Lord, and you will never be the same. Open the door that separates you from the Lord and let Him in. Do not wait, because no one knows the numbers of their days and making this decision is everything when it comes to eternity with or without God.

The Lord Is the Good Shepherd

One weekend while we were at our family cabin, I was reading the very last section of the very last chapter titled "Great Expectations" of the book *"Radical Reliance: Living 24/7 with God at the Center"* written by Joseph M. Stowell. The message was how God satisfies our souls, sustains our lives, and secures us in even great danger. The lesson cited the **Psalms of David: Psalms 23** about the **"Lord as our Shepherd."**

After reading through this section about the analogy of God as the **Good Shepherd**, I then decided I might read my Bible a little before turning in for the night. Something incredible happened next. I reached for the Bible on the end table behind my head, as I was lying down on the couch. I grabbed the Bible behind me and with no searching or anything, my thumb went to hold the Bible from a center page and the Bible fell open. I looked down on the page it fell open randomly to and with great astonishment, I read from **John 10:1** with the heading **"The Good Shepherd and His Sheep."** In this section Christ outlines to His disciples how He is like the Good Shepherd caring for His flock—and just like **Psalms 23**, **John 10:1-2** says: *Verily, verily, I say unto you, He that entereth not by the door into the sheepfold, but climbeth up some other way, the same is a thief and a robber. But he that entereth in by the door is the shepherd of the sheep.* Being stunned and comforted are the only words I can use to describe my reaction to this experience.

After returning home from our cabin, my first daily email devotional popped up about The Good Shepherd and His sheep from the same verse **John 10:1**—it was both awesome and confirming.

Incredible—Everyday!

It has almost become a common occurrence that I will read a Bible verse in a book somewhere and the same identical verse will come up again in the same day randomly in an email devotional, or another different book I am reading. It is fairly frequent and unexplainable. For example, once I was reading from the book titled: *"Journey to the Mountain of God"* by David D. Ireland which was about **Romans 8:18-25** and then I received a random daily devotional email containing the same verses from the Bible, **Romans 8:18-25.** What are the chances of that exactly, given all the many different verses in the Bible? I am not sure. Here were the verses I had read in both places in the same day:

Romans 8:18-25: Future Glory *For, I reckon that the sufferings of this present time are not worthy to be compared with the glory which shall be revealed in us. For the earnest expectation of the creature waiteth for the manifestation of the sons of God. For the creature was made subject to vanity, not willingly, but by reason of him who hath subjected the same in hope, Because the creature itself also shall be delivered from the bondage of corruption into the glorious liberty of the children of God. For we know that the whole creation groaneth and travaileth in pain together until now. And not only they, but ourselves also, which have the first fruits of the Spirit, even we ourselves groan within ourselves, waiting for the adoption, to wit, the redemption of our body. For we are saved by hope: but hope that is seen is not hope: for what a man seeth, why doth he yet hope for? But if we hope for that we see not, then do we with patience wait for it.*

Perseveres

Ethan and I are involved in a puppet ministry program, and the group uses lots of props and puppets for large shows involving a group of 30 or more people and we often travel to different churches with the group. I was assigned a group of props for a new puppet show and one prop was a sign that simply said the word: **"PERSEVERES."** Right after being assigned the **"Perseveres"** word sign prop one night, the next morning, I turned to my daily Bible devotions from a book called *"Journey to the Mountain of God"* by David D. Ireland, and the section I was reading that day had a heading titled **"Perseveres"** and it was all about the perseverance of the Christian with a focus on the verse **James 1:12** saying: *blessed is the man who perseveres under trial.* This was incredible, considering I had just spent the entire night before, thinking about the meaning of the word "Perseveres" all because of the show prop I was assigned with the same word.

Chapter Thirteen—Electricity

Electrical Shocks

Now when I was younger I would still go home to visit my parents, even though I lived in an apartment elsewhere. I was staying in a twin bed in my parent's spare bedroom and one morning something incredible happened to me. I felt myself bolt out of bed. I did not fall out of bed—I was thrown clear of the bed. At the time this happened, I had the incredible sensation that I had experienced some kind of an electrical shock.

This experience left me puzzled and perplexed for many years. I know what I experienced and I even explained to my parents at the time that I did not fall out of bed that I was literally thrown clear of it about a foot and that it was as if I had felt some sort of an electrical shock at the time.

I never forgot this mysterious experience over the years. One day, many years later, I was amazed when I read about someone else telling of having an encounter with Christ and that it was as if this person experienced the sensation of an electrical charge during their encounter. This completely intrigued me. I decided to research this phenomenon and then next I found an account of a woman who was blind. She was thrown clear of her bed and she felt some sort of an electrical shock. She regained her vision through a miraculous healing during that experience. While at our church camp, I had read in a book that the author he had an angelic visitation in which he also experienced a kind of electric shock when the angel's hands touched him. Then in my further research, I even came across two more reports both from pastors who experienced very similar electrical shock sensations. One pastor gave a description that he actually felt the presence of the Lord as if waves of electrical current were running through him. The other pastor described Christ appearing to him, Jesus touched the pastor's shoulders, and he too experienced a kind of electrical current flowing to himself from Christ. As I read all of these accounts, I was intrigued because I had never forgotten the experience I had had that one morning. I had begun wondering if there was not some connection to these other reports of electrical shocks in conjunction with miraculous activities and the *presence of the Lord.* I will never forget what happened to me before. Clearly, I had felt some sort of electrical shock, but I was nowhere near any source of electricity in any form at the time.

My family had gone to the Sunday morning service at our church camp and the memory of what I had read in the book about the author's electrical sensation during his angelic visitation was still fresh on my mind. In fact, during the Sunday service the thought came to my mind about my experience of bolting out of bed and feeling as if I had been shocked in some way. I had a little note pad and pen with me during the church service. I was planning to journal my thoughts about the *"electricity"* experience that I noted others had and I wrote the word *"electricity"* on the pad of paper in quote marks.

The next thing that happened was surreal. My son was looking on when he saw me write the single word ***"ELECTRICITY"*** on the pad of paper in my hand. I had no idea what our church camp pastor was about to say in his message. To my amazement, the next thing the pastor speaking had said was that God brought down the lightning—then he proceeded to say that Ben Franklin took that lightning and generated ***"ELECTRICITY."*** There was no tip off that his sermon was heading this direction at all when I had written that word ***"ELECTRICITY"*** down. There was also no space of time between the two events. I had written down the word ***"ELECTRICITY"*** and that was the next thing the pastor discussed. Even my son, who was sitting next to me at the time, saw it happen and he was amazed that I had written the word just prior to the pastor speaking about electricity. I wondered if this was some kind of confirmation about the amazing experience I had years before, that indeed it was an encounter with God. It was another amazing event. I have since actually heard a minister on TV talking about a woman she knew whose shoulder was healed miraculously. She too, reported feeling an electrical shock in her shoulder at the time of the healing and the minister was amazed.

And They Found Dry Land

On my own, I packed up the car and headed out for a two-hour drive to join my family already at our family cabin at our church camp. On the way, I spent time talking to the Lord. After declaring my love for Christ, for some reason I decided to turn the radio on to find something interesting. I came across a minister speaking about God parting the Red Sea for Moses and the Israelites when they were trying to escape captivity from the Egyptians and how God takes care of His own.

As I am hearing about the Israelites on the radio, suddenly a huge rainstorm blows up while I am driving. The rain became so heavy that I could hardly see a foot in front of my car. Then even more rapidly than the way the rain suddenly came down on me, I drove right out of the rain into complete dryness with absolutely no rain at all. I looked in my rearview mirror and marveled at how quickly this big rain had disappeared. It was almost as if a faucet had been turned completely off. I could actually see a giant wall of water behind me. At the exact moment, my car moved out of the wall of rain into complete dryness, the minister on the radio who was preaching about the Israelites and the parting of the Red Sea said the words, **"And they found dry land."** I immediately thought to myself, (*as I pulled out of a wall of rain into complete dryness*) "Did that minister just say, **'And they found dry land?'**" I was stunned—the exact instant the radio pastor said, *"And they found dry land"—I had found dry land!* It was overwhelming.

Exodus 14:22: *And the Israelites went through the sea on dry ground, with a wall of water on their right and on their left.*

Capturing My Heart

While traveling on a two-lane highway, I was talking to God as I often do when I am alone in the car. I declared aloud to God that *"I was out to capture His heart"* and I was driving at the bottom of a hill at the time heading to the top of the hill. I no longer had those words out of my mouth to God as I crested the top of the hill at that exact moment I saw, not one, but two gigantic heart-shaped signs. To tell God I was out to capture His heart only to look up and see two giant heart-shaped signs at that next moment caused me to laugh. This was either the most incredibly timed coincidence or something else—I choose to believe that God can orchestrate such wonderful detailed events because I know that God is in charge of all the details of our lives.

God Laughs

The Bible speaks of God's sense of humor in several places and I just want to say that on more than one occasion I am sure there is laughter in Heaven over my reaction to something that God is doing in my life. One such day came at lunchtime. I was home alone and talking aloud to the Holy Spirit and I stated with all sorts of authority that I was recently reading how the Holy Spirit is the most ignored of the Trinity: Father, Son, and Holy Spirit. In addition, I was addressing the Holy Spirit about how I felt so bad about this statement and I for one wanted to do a better job of not ignoring the Holy Spirit. Then I said to the Holy Spirit, "You know, you do come and live with us forever." Then, I stated that I knew that because I read it in the Bible somewhere, but I could not exactly remember where I had read it.

Well do you know at that next moment, I sat down to eat a bowl of soup for lunch and I opened the book I had been reading, which was all about God. At that moment, I turned to the next the page to the exact verse I had just referred to aloud regarding the Holy Spirit (*the very same one that I told the Holy Spirit I could not remember where it was in the Bible*) and I nearly spit the soup out all over the table in front of me. To say I was in shock or greatly surprised would have been an understatement. I know that the Holy Spirit had to be chuckling at my amazement to turn to the *very verse* I was just quoting (even though I was unable to recall where it was located). Here is that verse, by the way:

John 14:15-17: *If ye love me, keep my commandments. And I will pray the Father, and he shall give you another Comforter, that he may abide with you forever; Even the Spirit of truth; whom the world cannot receive, because it seeth him not, neither knoweth him: ye know him; for he dwelleth with you, and shall be in you.*

Yes, I have discovered that God has a marvelous sense of humor and to believe otherwise is just not Biblical. The Bible describes God on more than one occasion of partaking in laughter and that He is a most happy God. This should bring a great sense of peace and comfort to us that God is fun loving and it brings me great happiness to know this is true. He has given His creation a sense of humor, laughter, and the understanding of joy. Joy is one of the fruits of the Spirit and I do not know of how one can really experience joy without laughter. I have experienced many times in which God has brought me sheer joy and laughter and this was one of those occasions. Part of true friendship is sharing joy and laughter together, don't you think? I feel no differently about my relationship with God.

Psalms 37:12-13: *The wicked plotteth against the just, and gnasheth upon him with his teeth. The LORD shall laugh at him: for he seeth that his day is coming.*

Psalms 2:4: *He that sitteth in the heavens shall laugh: the LORD shall have them in derision.*

Proverbs 18:21

I have been helping a friend with a new project completely inspired by God. My friend, Princess LaVear, was experiencing some depression and she decided to create her own self-talk CDs based on Bible scripture verses for her own personal use. They turned out to be tremendously helpful to her so she decided to research and find out if anyone had them and to order or purchase more of them for her own use. In her research, she could not find any at all. Then one morning the Lord spoke to my friend and told her that there were no self-talk scripture-based CDs and He wanted her to make them. So, my friend decided to create these CDs for others to use.

She developed some self-help, self-talk CDs that are the first-ever Bible-based like them. I was up late one night working on a press release for this project. And I was using the same verse that my friend uses at her website to promote the CDs: **Proverbs 18:21**. Here is the opening paragraph of the press release I was writing:

The self-talk self-help Industry has already been using the techniques the Bible describes in **Proverbs 18:21:** *Death and life are in the power of the tongue: and they that love it shall eat the fruit thereof.*

Well I worked on that press release until late at night and then the next morning, I flipped on my laptop and checked my email. Then my usual daily email devotional arrived first thing. Never do I know what message will arrive on my daily devotional email. I opened it and was shocked—it was all about **Proverbs 18:21**—the same verse I was using in the press release I was writing just the night before. This was a tremendous confirmation from the Lord for the work we were doing I believe. To learn more about these Self-Talk from the Scriptures™ CDs, visit www.Berenewed.com.

Chapter Fourteen—God's Message

God's Message

Back when I was doing some of my research on the topic of Heaven, I ran across Retha McPherson's story of her family and book titled *"A Message from God"* telling how they were all involved in a terrible car accident. The year of her family's car accident, she had become the reigning Mrs. South Africa. Her two boys, two-year-old Josh and twelve-year-old Aldo were thrown clear of their vehicle. In this remarkable story, Aldo has the fight for his life in a coma state from brain damage. Although their youngest was fine, their lives are turned upside down over night. Retha described having an experience where she is taken to the throne of God while praying in the hospital for the very life of her oldest child. Her oldest son meanwhile is in a coma state, having a near-death experience in Heaven meeting Jesus.

When her son Aldo finally miraculously recovers from a coma, and the hospital staff give no hope that he will be past age two in mentality. Although unable to speak, Aldo later can only handwrite messages to his Mother and they discover that he is himself and not the mental age of a two-year-old. In fact, he is so much more. Even though only 12-years-old and formerly only interested in soccer and Playstation™, Aldo miraculously commands knowledge of God and the Bible adults wish they knew. He reveals many of the amazing things he learns while visiting Christ and Heaven during his near-death experience as well. His incredible knowledge of God and Bible verse memorization are way beyond that of a typical 12-year-old, revealing the miracle of his personal testimony. As the reigning Mrs. South Africa, Retha was easily recognized in her home country further demonstrating her credible witness.

Because of my research, Retha and I became friends and communicated often and she wanted to tell her story abroad, because God told her this story would go around the world (and it has). I offered to help her get media exposure and to help with editing the book. Retha had informed me she needed help promoting her book in the states and I offered to help her if she wanted my help. Soon after, I felt God is leading me to help Retha in the U.S. and I arranged for her to do TV and radio interviews while in the states. Retha flew to the U.S. and stayed with me one week while I took her to South Bend, Indiana for the taping of the Internationally syndicated "Harvest TV Show."

The morning we were to go to an early morning taping of the "Harvest Show," we were staying at a hotel near the studio. That morning in the hotel, Retha said that God had spoken a word of scripture to her. He gave her **Ephesians 4:1-5**. When she did not do it right away, He even reminded her a second time to go to the Bible and to read the verse. Well together, we looked up the verse not knowing what we would find. After receiving that blessing we went on to the show and after Retha's interview, we received a tour of the television studio and went back to the guest waiting room to watch the remainder of the show. That is when we received an amazing surprise.

The TV show's daily message at the tail end of the same show of Retha's interview was on included the reading of the same verse **Ephesians 4:1-5**. This was the identical verse we received from God to read *BEFORE* we ever left the hotel to do the show. We were amazed, blessed, and received an incredible confirmation that God's mighty hand was at work as always. Here is that amazing verse we received from the Lord—before the show and after the interview had been taped:

Ephesians 4:1-5: *I therefore, the prisoner of the Lord, beseech you that ye walk worthy of the vocation wherewith ye are called, With all lowliness and meekness, with longsuffering, forbearing one another in love; Endeavouring to keep the unity of the Spirit in the bond of peace. There is one body, and one Spirit, even as ye are called in one hope of your calling; One Lord, one faith, one baptism.*

The night before the taping of the "Harvest Show" in our hotel near the studio, I woke up in the middle of the night, I saw this bright light streak past me making a half-circle arc, and it looked like a tiny shooting star next to the bed. I looked again and could not see it or any other light source in the room at all, and so I went back to sleep. The next morning, I mentioned seeing the light streaking in the dark to Retha and she said that she never sees these herself, but her youngest son Josh who was then a six-year-old, sees them often at home. She said that it was an angel and these things happen frequently to them at home ever since having their miraculous visits with the Lord.

After coming back from South Bend, Indiana from the "Harvest Show" taping the next morning, on a Friday at 3:00 a.m., I took Retha McPherson and her business partner Manie Du Toit to the airport across town to fly out of Indianapolis, Indiana. I then came home and took my son to school and returned our rental car and then a good friend brought me back home. After all that running around, I laid down and rested from sheer exhaustion from all the busyness of the past few days. Amazingly, I heard the Lord speak in that still small gentle voice and He whispered to me, *"We are precious in His sight."*

On the following Monday morning, when I had my first chance to do my usual Bible study, I decided to read from the book of Ephesians because of what had just happened during the Harvest TV Show. Because of the amazing confirmation we received with the verse God gave to Retha in the hotel room that morning, I decided to go back to reread **Ephesians 4:1-5**. I started reading Ephesians and amazingly, I read the first commentary notes in the Ephesians section of my Bible and the copy *"We are precious in His sight"* was in the commentary I came to. Now remember, just the Friday before the Lord had spoken these very words to me after I came home and collapsed on the bed from being up late taking Retha and Manie to the airport. I felt this was a wonderful confirmation to the incredible message I had received from the Lord.

I really had felt the Lord's heart-warming presence when I heard those beautiful words. In **1 Kings 19:10-13**, the Bible tells the amazing story of Elijah and how he heard the voice of the Lord as a whisper in the same way I had heard Him:

1 Kings 19:10-13: *And he said, I have been very jealous for the LORD God of hosts: for the children of Israel have forsaken thy covenant, thrown down thine altars, and slain thy prophets with the sword; and I, even I only, am left; and they seek my life, to take it away. And he said, Go forth, and stand upon the mount before the LORD. And, behold, the LORD passed by, and a great and strong wind rent the mountains, and brake in pieces the rocks before the LORD; but the LORD was not in the wind: and after the wind an earthquake; but the LORD was not in the earthquake: And after the earthquake a fire; but the LORD was not in the fire: and after the fire* ***a still small voice.*** *And it was so, when Elijah heard it, that he wrapped his face in his mantle, and went out, and stood in the entering in of the cave. And, behold, there came a voice unto him, and said, What doest thou here, Elijah?*

A couple months later, Retha returned to the states to do a half-hour episode on the syndicated TV show "It's Supernatural!™ & Messianic Vision" hosted by Sid Roth including a dramatic actor-re-enactment of their tragic accident. I had arranged with the TV show for Retha's story and her book to be featured. *"A Message from God"* was received so well when it first aired to an International syndicated audience, that the TV show sold 800 copies the first day of the program aired. The "Messianic Vision" TV show staff also put out a newsletter by email to the show's newsletter mailing list and they mentioned *"A Message from God"* in that newsletter and an additional 900 copies sold from just that mailing alone.

Retha's television episode on "It's Supernatural!™ & Messianic Vision" sold so many books that it required several reprints to keep up with the demand of the TV audience and the staff reported that it sold more books than any of their other interviewed guests during that entire year.

The show also entered Retha's episode in a television awards program and her interview on the half-hour TV show won a Television Angel Award. "It's Supernatural!™ & Messianic Vision" received an Angel Award for the amazing interview with Retha McPherson. The Angel Award is given by Excellence in Media, "an organization dedicated to the promotion of quality family-oriented programming in all facets of communication." Silver Angels are awarded to productions that are professional and have had the highest moral, spiritual, ethical, or social impact. I know that this family's life has been turned upside down by these experiences but they are on a mission to reach people to Christ through their story and book *"A Message from God."*

Same Message, Same Week

God spoke to me through a unique experience related to Retha McPherson. To tell you what happened next, let me first tell you about another good friend of mine. I have a good friend, Princess LaVear, who was interested in the format of Self-Talk, which is used primarily by a secular and self-help audience through the concept of positive reinforcement on audio CDs. Princess LaVear created her own Scripture-based self-talk CDs and enjoyed the benefit of them. She went online to find more to order and could find none. Then early one morning, the Lord spoke to her saying that there was no Scripture-based Self-Talk format CDs and He wanted her to create them for people to use. She created a prototype version and a website to promote it.

In the fall of 2007, I had spoken to Retha McPherson about helping her promote her book in the U.S. and Internationally on Amazon, the largest online worldwide bookseller. At the same time, I had offered to help Princess LaVear promote her Self-Talk from the Scriptures™ CDs. At that time both women were busy with other endeavors and they told me that they would get in touch with me later. After the 2007 Christmas Holidays, one week in mid-January, Retha called me from South Africa excitedly and said she had been visiting Rwanda, Africa with her family over Christmas vacation. She told me that the Lord had spoken to her and told her to promote her book soon and that once she did He would be coming soon after. She called to see if I would help her to get her book up on Amazon as I had suggested I could do earlier that fall. She was earnestly excited by her message from the Lord to get the book out soon.

Within the space of a couple days of Retha's call from South Africa, I received a second call from my friend Princess LaVear in California who told me that the Lord had spoken to her and she was told by Him to get her CD project out soon because He would be coming soon after the CDs come out. She too was very anxious to get her project underway and was getting ready to make urgent preparations to begin producing multiple versions of her Self-Talk from the Scriptures™ CDs.

Now these two women had not spoken to each other nor did they know each other to speak to each other. Yet they both call me within a couple days of each other—with virtually the same message—to get their books and CDs out into the general public's hands and that soon after Christ would be coming. They were both excited about their requests to me. You could hear incredible urgency in their voices as they both pled their cases on each call. I was quite stunned by this event and took it at as a serious word to me as well that both women would call me within a couple days with essentially the same message. I want to add that because of their great geographic distance from me, I normally communicate with them each by email. Rarely, does either one ever call me or in this instance, they both called me on the phone. *Retha McPherson's book can be found at www.Rethamcpherson.com and Princess LaVear's Self-Talk from the Scriptures™ CDs can be found at www.berenewed.com.*

Ephesians 2:10: *For we are his workmanship, created in Christ Jesus unto good works, which God hath before ordained that we should walk in them.*

Amos 3:7

My son Ethan went to a friend's birthday party and several of his friends' Moms were also at the party. A couple of the Moms at this party were friends and we spent some time talking while the party was going on. I spoke to them about the many different amazing spiritual experiences I was having. Then I told them that the Lord was continually showing me in a variety of ways and through different people that *He is coming soon*. I also told them that I put this information out of my mind, but incredibly, the Lord keeps bringing it back into my focus repeatedly. In addition, I told these Moms that *it dawned on me one day that wouldn't you tell your best friend what it is you are going to do before you do it?*

After our conversation, one of the Moms left the party to go out to eat dinner. Then a little while later, the Mom who left the party to go eat, came back and ran towards me with great obvious enthusiasm. Then she told me she had something very important to tell me. She proceeded to tell me that before we had ever spoken at all, on her way to the party in the first place, that she had a Bible verse that kept going through her mind repeatedly. She said to me that she knew that that verse was especially meant to be delivered to me. She told me it was **Amos 3:7**. And then she recited the verse that had been going through her mind repeatedly before she arrived to the party:

Amos 3:7: *Surely the Lord GOD will do nothing, but he revealeth his secret unto his servants the prophets.*

I was astonished at the similarity between what I had said before she told me this with the verse she gave me. It was confirming about all the times I knew the Lord had been showing me that He is coming soon and *we are into the season of the Lord's return.*

The Soon Return of Christ

I was once talking to a close family member on the phone and I told this person that I believed that Christ was coming soon. This person swiftly reminded me that my Grandmother believed that Christ was coming soon too during World War I and World War II and that Christ did not come then and He was not coming now. I was crushed to hear this considering the many ways Christ was showing me *He is coming soon.*

Now I know that many Christians believe this way. I thought about these words and how my Grandmother faithfully followed and watched for Christ. My earthly Father, who has since passed away, also watched for Christ ardently during his lifetime. I thought about the very first Christians from the New Testament and how they too watched for Christ's return.

What did my dear Grandmother…my Dad…and the early New Testament Christians all have in common? Well apart from the fact that they have all since passed away—they all watched *and longed* for the promised return of Jesus and the catching away of the saints to the New Jerusalem as outlined in the Bible. It does not matter that none of them lived during the time of the generation that would actually see the return of Christ and the rapture, they all would still earn the Crown of Righteousness as promised to them in the Bible. *Did you catch that?* God accounts that watching for the return of Christ as being so significant that *He awards a crown to the watcher in the next life.* **This is the mandate of God for the follower of Christ to watch for His return to take home His Bride.** Here is the verse regarding the Crown of Righteousness:

2 Timothy 4:8: *Henceforth there is laid up for me a crown of righteousness, which the Lord, the righteous judge, shall give me at that day: and not to me only, but unto all them also that love his appearing.*

So many Christians are caught up in the things of the world and when you even suggest watching for the soon coming of Jesus, I hear so frequently their response from the verse **Matthew 24:36:** *But of that day and hour knoweth no man, no, not the angels of heaven, but my Father only.* So they excuse themselves by saying that since only the Father knows the day and time of these things, then let's not worry or talk about it. Only, here is the actual section in the Bible with this verse:

Matthew 24:36-44: *But of that day and hour knoweth no man, no, not the angels of heaven, but my Father only. But as the days of Noah were, so shall also the coming of the Son of man be. For as in the days that were before the flood they were eating and drinking, marrying and giving in marriage, until the day that Noah entered into the ark, And knew not until the flood came, and took them all away; so shall also the coming of the Son of man be. Then shall two be in the field; the one shall be taken, and the other left. Two women shall be grinding at the mill; the one shall be taken, and the other left.* **Watch therefore: for ye know not what hour your Lord doth come.** *But know this, that if the goodman of the house had known in what watch the thief would come,* **he would have watched,** *and would not have suffered his house to be broken up.* **Therefore be ye also ready: for in such an hour as ye think not the Son of man cometh.**

This verse essentially says that *BECAUSE* no one knows about that day or hour, therefore keep watch. *BECAUSE* you do not know on what day or hour your Lord will come *you need to watch.* This verse is frequently misquoted and misused to say because no one knows about the day or hour but only the Father, so then just put it out of your mind. Now let us read further into this section of the Bible:

Matthew 24:45-51: *Who then is a faithful and wise servant, whom his lord hath made ruler over his household, to give them meat in due season? Blessed is that servant, whom his lord when he cometh shall find so doing. Verily I say unto you, That he shall make him ruler over all his goods. But and if that evil servant shall say in his heart, My lord delayeth his coming; And shall begin to smite his fellow servants, and to eat and drink with the drunken; The lord of that servant shall come in a day when he looketh not for him, and in an hour that he is not aware of, And shall cut him asunder, and appoint him his portion with the hypocrites: there shall be weeping and gnashing of teeth.*

Here then are some sobering words from the Bible that the master will come on a day when He is not expected and an hour He is not looked for and the servant not looking for the Master will be assigned to a place with the hypocrites.

Now when the signs of the soon return of Christ start to happen, *and they are now*, then how much more important is it for this generation to be watching for Christ? Therefore, God says that He will reward those who diligently watch for and long for the return of Christ. *God will punish those who do not watch for Christ* and occupy themselves with other pursuits. Now with the events foretold to happen at the soon coming of Christ for His Bride taking place now, it is shameful for Christians not to be looking for Christ's soon return. In addition, it is shameful for Christians to persecute and condemn those who are faithfully looking and watching especially since this is what the Bible specifically prescribes *for all true followers of Christ.*

The Crown of Righteousness (awarded for those who long for His appearing) is called this for two main reasons. One reason is that it is the *hope and inspiration* of the Christians' during a time of great darkness and life's struggles to watch for Christ's return. The other reason is that when Christians watch and anticipate Christ's return to retrieve His Church they are more inclined to pursue holiness and "righteousness" in anticipation of the near coming of the Lord. When people believe that Jesus' coming is close, they tend to *surrender* their lives to Christ and to turn from evil in the only way it is possible to pursue holiness—through Christ.

Hebrews 9:27-28: *And as it is appointed unto men once to die, but after this the judgment: So Christ was once offered to bear the sins of many; and unto them that look for him shall he appear the second time without sin unto salvation.*

Power by Faith
One morning when I first woke up and before I could form any thoughts of my own, I heard from the Lord the words, *"Power by Faith"* and I thought, okay what does this mean? *Later that same night,* I was reading from a book that had a section that spoke all about *Power by Faith.* Faith in God brings us His power to accomplish His will. Here are some verses about power by faith:

1 Peter 1:3-5: *Blessed be the God and Father of our Lord Jesus Christ, which according to his abundant mercy hath begotten us again unto a lively hope by the resurrection of Jesus Christ from the dead, To an inheritance incorruptible, and undefiled, and that fadeth not away, reserved in heaven for you,* **Who are kept by the power of God through faith unto salvation ready to be revealed in the last time.**

2 Thessalonians 1:11: *Wherefore also we pray always for you, that our God would count you worthy of this calling, and fulfill all the good pleasure of his goodness,* **and the work of faith with power:**

1 Corinthians 2:4-5: *And my speech and my preaching was not with enticing words of man's wisdom, but in demonstration of the Spirit and of power:* **That your faith should not stand in the wisdom of men, but in the power of God.**

How Will We Be Remembered?
Over a lunch meeting with my best friend, who is a nurse in outpatient surgery, she told me how she had been talking with a patient having surgery recently. This patient told her about his near-death experiences he had and one time he was out of his body with God and God was reviewing his entire life in front of him—then he came back to life. He said he was not afraid of death because he knew where he was going.

After lunch, in my car ride home, I was talking to God and saying that I hope that there will be good things about my life. Unbelievably, as soon as I got home, I opened my incoming email and my daily devotion popped up, and it asked, *"How will you be remembered?"*—"How will your life be remembered?"

God's Robe

During one of my morning prayer times (and remember prayer is just talking with God), I spoke to God of touching the hem of His robe and I actually referred to the time in the Bible that the woman who was ill for a long time went seeking after Christ who came through her neighborhood. She could not get past the throng of people around Christ to get to Him, but in faith, she reached out and simply touched the hem of His robe. Christ stopped and told His disciples that He knew someone had touched the hem of His robe. He asked who had touched His robe. The woman spoke up and said that she had touched His robe and Jesus said that her faith had healed her.

Luke 8:42-48: *For he had one only daughter, about twelve years of age, and she lay a dying. But as he went the people thronged him. And a woman having an issue of blood twelve years, which had spent all her living upon physicians, neither could be healed of any, Came behind him, and touched the border of his garment: and immediately her issue of blood stanched. And Jesus said, Who touched me? When all denied, Peter and they that were with him said, Master, the multitude throng thee and press thee, and sayest thou, Who touched me? And Jesus said, somebody hath touched me: for I perceive that virtue is gone out of me. And when the woman saw that she was not hid, she came trembling, and falling down before him, she declared unto him before all the people for what cause she had touched him, and how she was healed immediately. And he said unto her, Daughter, be of good comfort: thy faith hath made thee whole; go in peace.*

During this prayer, I requested that I too wanted to touch the hem of the robe of God.

Within the same day of praying this prayer later on, three separate descriptions of the robe of the Lord came my way arbitrarily from three completely, unique sources. One came during my daily devotional reading and another was from an online description about a book I was thinking about checking out of the library about God. The third amazing encounter happened while I was waiting in my car to pick up my son from school. I randomly picked up a book about God I had in my car (I had not actually even been recently reading this particular book). I decided to turn to a section in the book that spoke exactly about the robes of Christ—I was dumbstruck.

First, this particular reference came up in my daily email devotions in which the woman who touched Jesus' robe was referenced.

The second reference to God's robe amazingly came up when I was looking for a book to check out, I read a random excerpt from a book online, which happened to be all about the description of the robe of God—all within a couple hours of my prayer. Although I was only interested in the book, the online book description included this verse reference about God's robe and a lengthy discussion about the beauty of His robe with this verse:

Isaiah 6:1: *In the year that king Uzziah died I saw also the LORD sitting upon a throne, high and lifted up, and his train filled the temple (or his robe filled the temple).*

The third reference was from a book I grabbed in my car to look at while I was killing time waiting to pick up my son. When I opened the book randomly, I immediately turned to the author's reference to the robe of the Lord.

Quite honestly, I do not ever remember a time that I had seen so many references to God's robe in one day as the day I had referred to touching His robe in my morning prayer. I just could not help to be amazed by running into three references of the Lord's robe after personally requesting to touch His robe in my prayer. That day I felt I had actually touched His robe.

Chapter Fifteen—Grains of Sand

Grains of Sand

Praying and talking to God in my car was getting to be so important to me. I really value my time in the car alone where I can chat with the Lord about things going on in my life. Sometimes I speak of my concerns of the day, sometimes I tell the Lord how much I appreciate Him, and other times I would wax philosophical about something. While traveling to pick up my son from school one day, I was asking what God was thinking about me before He created me. Suddenly in a clear soft-spoken voice, I heard very simply the words, **"Grains of sand."** It was both startling and incredible to hear this from the Lord. I knew the words He spoke were familiar to me as from the Bible, but just the same, I rushed home to look these words up for myself in the Bible. The verses containing this phrase in the Bible are found in and the phrase the Lord gave me had answered my question completely.

Psalms 139:15-18: *My substance was not hid from thee, when I was made in secret, and curiously wrought in the lowest parts of the earth. Thine eyes did see my substance, yet being imperfect; and in thy book all my members were written, which continuance were fashioned, when as yet there was none of them. **How precious also are thy thoughts unto me, O God! How great is the sum of them! If I should count them, they are more in number than the sand: when I awake, I am still with thee.***

About one month or so later, we were visiting the beautiful and new Creation Museum located in Petersburg, Kentucky across the river from Cincinnati, Ohio. We had visited the museum's planetarium program and they were illustrating the vastness of the universe on the ceiling and where exactly the earth fits in with all the other millions of stars in space.

For no real reason while I was watching this program, the memory came back to me about the time God had spoken of how His thoughts of me would outnumber the *"Grains of sand."* IMMEDIATELY after I had recalled God speaking to me the words *"Grains of sand,"* the narrator of the planetarium program commented that the stars were numbered like the *"Grains of sand."* Of course, I did not know that my memory of hearing the Lord say *"Grains of sand"* would be echoed by the narrator of the planetarium program within moments apart. It was yet another outstanding confirmation of the time before when I had asked the Lord about what His thoughts were of me before He created me. Even though I experienced this dazzling display of God's abilities, I can scarcely take it all in.

Hebrews 11:12: *Therefore sprang there even of one, and him as good as dead, so many as the stars of the sky in multitude, and as the sand which is by the sea shore innumerable.*

At one point in time, we did not exist at all. Then at another point in time, we were merely a thought in the mind of God. Then God created us and amazingly we now exist. I do not know about you, but I do not want to live outside the will of the One Who created me. I do not ever want to be apart from the One in Whose mind, at one point in time, I was just merely a thought.

Zephaniah 3:17

One morning, I read this verse on my daily email devotional:

Zephaniah 3:17: *The LORD thy God in the midst of thee is mighty; he will save, he will rejoice over thee with joy; you will rest in his love, he will joy over thee with singing.*

And I made special note of God singing…I was not aware that God sang over His people and that amazed me.

Then I was in my car that same afternoon waiting to pick up Ethan from his school. I grabbed a book I left in the car while I was waiting to pick up my son. I had not looked through this book for a while, because I left the book I had been reading at home. So, I randomly just turned to a page. And, you know what? It was **Zephaniah 3:17**! I remembered seeing that earlier on the devotional email on that same morning on the Internet. I thought to myself, there is that same exact verse again—all about God singing!

Then in the same day, I went home and picked up the book I had been reading and something amazing happened next. The chapter where I had last left off…right where I was getting ready to read…opened with the verse **Zephaniah 3:17**! The whole chapter I read next, referred to this particular verse throughout, in explaining the love of God for His people. What are the chances I should come across this one particular verse three times in the same day—in three separate unrelated locations—not just the whole book of Zephaniah from the Bible—this particular singular verse—wow! I had no idea that I would turn to this verse a third time.

As I am reading over this particular section again to edit it—I read with utter amazement again how I had ran across this one single verse—**Zephaniah 3:17**—three times randomly in a single day and I thought how wonderful that God should be so loving to do this for me! I pondered this wonderful thing through the night and even the next morning and it really warmed my heart just thinking of it.

As soon as I was able that morning, I turned to my Bible and looked up **Zephaniah 3:17** and reread it. That same day I was pondering about the wonder of seeing **Zephaniah 3:17** three times in the same day, and I was home and reading still yet a third book and I had not been so far into the book but turned to a page, which quoted the verse **Zephaniah 3:17** again after pondering this all night and morning. Once again, I ran into this wonderful amazing verse. Could this just be a wonderful happen chance again? The logical thinking person may refute such a thing—but a joyful person who loves God and views Him to be most loving must embrace such a thing from faith. All things supernatural like healings, miracles, hearing from God, signs and wonders require faith to believe in them—all things from God require faith because He *IS* supernatural.

In **John 20:24-31:** it is written: *But Thomas, one of the twelve, called Didymus, was not with them when Jesus came. The other disciples therefore said unto him, We have seen the Lord. But he said unto them, Except I shall see in his hands the print of the nails, and put my finger into the print of the nails, and thrust my hand into his side, I will not believe. And after eight days again his disciples were within, and Thomas with them: then came Jesus, the doors being shut, and stood in the midst, and said, Peace be unto you. Then saith he to Thomas, Reach hither thy finger, and behold my hands; and reach hither thy hand, and thrust it into my side: and be not faithless, but believing. And Thomas answered and said unto him, My Lord and my God. Jesus saith unto him, Thomas, because thou hast seen me, thou hast believed: blessed are they that have not seen, and yet have believed. And many other signs truly did Jesus in the presence of his disciples, which are not written in this book: But these are written, that ye might believe that Jesus is the Christ, the Son of God; and that believing ye might have life through his name.*

God Is Everywhere

When this happened my son, Ethan was eleven and "all boy." Nevertheless, he also has a very sensitive side to him. Recently, with all seriousness, while we were in the car talking, he told me the most extraordinary thing. He said that God revealed some insight about Himself to Ethan. Ethan said to me, "You know how God is everywhere all of the time?" I agreed and he said that God had revealed how He is everywhere all the time to him…and he proceeded to ask me, "You know how God is light?" I agreed with this statement. "Well everywhere light is—God is," he continued. I then asked him, "Well, what about where the darkness is?" He answered immediately with automatic precision, "Well God makes light we can't see." I thought about this and I wondered how would a child have such profound insight about God in which he was given zero time to prepare such an answer? I came upon these Bible verses, which I am quite sure Ethan did not have foreknowledge, which only confirms what was revealed to him about God. I do believe that God revealed this information to him:

Psalms 139:7-12: *Whither shall I go from thy spirit? Or whither shall I flee from thy presence? If I ascend up into heaven, thou art there: if I make my bed in hell, behold, thou art there. If I take the wings of the morning, and dwell in the uttermost parts of the sea; even there shall thy hand lead me, and thy right hand shall hold me.* ***If I say, surely the darkness shall cover me; even the night shall be light about me. Yea, the darkness hideth not from thee; but the night shineth as the day: the darkness and the light are both alike to thee.***

2 Corinthians 4:5-6: *For we preach not ourselves, but Christ Jesus the Lord; and ourselves your servants for Jesus' sake. For God, who commanded the light to shine out of darkness, hath shined in our hearts, to give the light of the knowledge of the glory of God in the face of Jesus Christ.*

James 1:17: *Every good gift and every perfect gift is from above, and cometh down from the* ***Father of lights,*** *with whom is no variableness, neither shadow of turning.*

1 John 1:5: *This then is the message which we have heard of him, and declare unto you, that God is light, and in him is no darkness at all.*

Isaiah 45:7: ***I form the light, and create darkness: I make peace, and create evil: I the LORD do all these things.***

Jeremiah 23:24: *Can any hide himself in secret places that I shall not see him? saith the LORD.* ***Do not I fill heaven and earth?*** *saith the LORD.*

Here Ethan tells what happened in his own words:
I was riding in the car coming on the way home from going out to eat at night and that reminded me to pray and I did and immediately after my prayer. I always say my prayers before dark because bad things happen in the dark and back then, I was always afraid of the dark. And immediately after I had finished my prayer God had put a thought into my head that He is light and light can go anywhere. Immediately I told my mom. I was never afraid of the dark ever again because I just picture God being there and He lights my way.

Chapter Sixteen—The Sparrow

The Sparrow

One morning as I first woke up and before I could process a single thought of my own, I heard the voice of the Lord speak these words: ***"His eye is on the sparrow and I know He watches me."*** Immediately I recognized this phrase as something I had heard before but definitely not recently. I had heard this in my distant past—so that I had to look it up because I could not recall if this was from the Bible or a music lyric or both. I did learn that it is a sacred gospel hymn. And, I was completely overwhelmed that the Lord would utter such incredibly sweet words to me. I know that people wonder what does the voice of the Holy Spirit sound like. All I can say is that whenever I have heard the audible voice of God it usually is a bit unsettling from the standpoint that it is never something that is predictable or anticipated for because it always comes, out-of-the-blue, without warning, and I absolutely never have any idea when it will happen.

The theme of this song is inspired by the words of Jesus in the Gospel of Matthew:

His Eye Is On the Sparrow

Verse 1
Why should I feel discouraged,
Why should the shadows come,
Why should my heart be lonely,
And long for Heaven and home,

When Jesus is my portion? My constant friend is He:
His eye is on the sparrow, and I know He watches me;
His eye is on the sparrow, and I know He watches me.

Refrain
I sing because I'm happy,
I sing because I'm free,
For His eye is on the sparrow,
And I know He watches me.

Verse 2
"Let not your heart be troubled," His tender word I hear,
And resting on His goodness, I lose my doubts and fears;
Though by the path He leadeth, but one step I may see;
His eye is on the sparrow, and I know He watches me;
His eye is on the sparrow, and I know He watches me.

Verse 3
Whenever I am tempted, whenever clouds arise,
When songs give place to sighing,
When hope within me dies,

I draw the closer to Him, from care He sets me free;
His eye is on the sparrow, and I know He watches me;
His eye is on the sparrow, and I know He watches me.

Matthew 6:26: *Behold the fowls of the air: for they sow not, neither do they reap, nor gather into barns; yet your heavenly Father feedeth them. Are ye not much better than they?*

About a year later, I was at a school play with my best friend and during the play, for some reason my mind wandered to the time I heard the Holy Spirit say the words to me, *"His eye is on the sparrow and I know He watches me."* There was nothing at all going on in the play to cause me to remember this experience. Yet, it was so amazing that I should ponder about the sparrow lyrics, because right after that the closing song in the play was the same hymn *"His Eye Is On the Sparrow!"*

God's eye is on us and there is great comfort in this, great comfort. We can depend on Him for everything—minute by minute. We can run our own lives into the ground—or we can surrender to the One who planned us, created us, died for us, cares for us, and who wants to live with us for all eternity. Even so, we spend so little time on this relationship with the One who made us. However, He gave us a whole book about Himself and some people never even open it or even own one.

When I think of the time I have spent apart from God, I feel such great regret. How I have hurt Him by my pursuit of everything but Him. As I write this, I hope you will give this some thought. What comes before God in your life...career, family, other relationships, wealth, position, hobbies, and entertainment? What things are more important to consume so much of your time? What you spend time focused on is what you worship. What you devote your time to is what you worship. What or who do you worship?

Matthew 22:36-40 says: *Master, which is the great commandment in the law? Jesus said unto him, "Thou shalt love the Lord thy God with all thy heart, and with all thy soul, and with thy mind. This is the first and great commandment, and the second is like unto it, Thou shalt love thy neighbor as thyself. On these two commandments hang all the law and the prophets.*

Six Hours*

Luke 23:44-46: *And it was about the sixth hour, and there was a darkness over all the earth until the ninth hour. And the sun was darkened and the veil of the temple was rent in the midst. And when Jesus had cried with a loud voice, he said, Father, into thy hands I commend my spirit: and having said thus, he gave up the ghost.*

The realization of exactly what Christ did for me on the cross came into stark focus one night. I had come across the verse in the Bible that tells the amount of time that Jesus was actually on the cross and it was six hours. This was a stunning thought to me and it really made me think about how He suffered. Never before, had I known this or had I even pondered that Jesus actually spent six hours up on the cross. It was hard to imagine how long He suffered and it is shocking to think that Christ lingered in this harsh way for six hours before dying for us.

Now please believe that never before had I really thought about Christ's incredible sacrifice of how He spent six hours on the cross. In addition, it really caught my attention and made me think of what He actually endured. About an hour after reading the Bible verse and realizing about the six-hour ordeal, we were playing a DVD movie about the study of the Star of Bethlehem and in the movie, the narrator comments about the six hours Christ was on the cross. I was surprised that within a short period of time I had heard two references to Christ's six hours of torment when previously I had not thought about this information at all. This is what He did for you.

*It is believed that Jesus was on the cross from 9 a.m. until 3 p.m.

Chapter Seventeen—The Art Museum

The Art Museum

Every year, my son and I make our traditional visit to the local art museum. This year was no different and we made our way through the first couple of floors of the museum all the way up to the top floor while looking around. We arrived at the top and to the contemporary art exhibit. We came to one wing in contemporary art and while strolling in we noticed a lot of strange art. Nevertheless, I went ahead of Ethan, moved on into the wing, and rounded the corner of the exhibit.

Before heading forward, I had noticed that the exhibit seemed to promote unusual festivals and the general overall theme seemed to glorify "rebellion." On one wall, there was a row of picket signs and one sign on display seemed to actually make fun of and blaspheme Jesus. Then as I headed around the corner to move further into this exhibit I have to tell you that I did not see a thing. I did not have a chance. It was as if I hit an invisible wall and I was overwhelmed by what came over me next. I felt a large sense of panic and an instantaneous need to cry and weep. To top it off, I became physically ill and nauseous in a way I have never experienced before in my life. I ran around the corner toward Ethan and I could not escape quickly enough.

As I approached Ethan, I only said to him that we needed to get out of there right now. Ethan did not question why I wanted to leave so suddenly because he seemed to understand my urgency to leave. Then the most amazing thing happened. Ethan stated that he was nauseous at the time I had approached him. This was also incredible, considering I had not yet told him that I was nauseous.

I have had a fear of heights and when I climb high towers or heights, I experience so much panic that my feet cramp up in pain. Well heading out of the museum, I was not experiencing any fear of heights but my feet cramped up in the same horrible way as if I was experiencing some horrible fearful thing. Remarkably, all I saw was the front of the exhibit—I never once saw anything else. Nevertheless, my stomach bubbled and churned in nausea for three days in a unique way I had never experienced in my entire life. Ethan's stomach bothered him for ten days. On the third day of my strange illness, I took communion and right after that I felt better and my illness subsided. Ethan also reported later that he had never had a nauseous stomach that felt the way that one did.

As Ethan and I headed out of the art museum that day, we went into a garden on the grounds to gather our composure. We both compared notes and determined that we were experiencing the same sickness and panic. I continued to have an overwhelming need to cry and I wept off and on the entire ride home in the car across town. As we sat in the art museum garden together, Ethan suddenly felt a warm hand touch the center of his back almost in a comforting way, but we saw no one with us. As we gathered our composure once in our car, Ethan and I decided that we would never come back to the art museum again. We had had a very frightening encounter and we both were convinced that it was demonic.

The museum display that seemed to glorify "rebellion" typifies everything that is counter to God. The Bible likens rebellion to witchcraft and the occult as explained in this verse in **1 Samuel 15:23:** *For rebellion is as the sin of witchcraft, and stubbornness is as iniquity and idolatry. Because thou hast rejected the word of the LORD, he hath also rejected thee from being king.*

This is what Ethan experienced that day at the art museum in his own words:

We had gone downtown to the art museum and we had gone through every exhibit except the modern exhibit on the top floor and I told my Mom this is kind of exciting until we got about 20 paces into the exhibit. I was looking at this little TV and the headphones I put on and I was kind of zoning out watching a movie. And then I saw my Mom walk ahead into the exhibit and then I got this gut feeling that sort of felt like my toes curled and my palms got sweaty and I felt like throwing up. She yelled at me to stop what I was doing and I did as she said. As she grabbed me by the arm, I looked back and saw this display of a dummy with a triangle box over the head, which got smaller until it ended at a point with a wheel at the bottom. The dummy was riding a bike. At that point, I wanted to run out. We went downstairs to get some food and then we took it to the park surrounding the museum there we prayed and we called my mom's best friend and we told her about it. Then on the way back home, I had gotten some free art museum tickets from school and I ripped them up and said to God that was for you. After that, I was sick at my stomach for a week and a half. It was not your normal stomachache.

Metal Buildings

Early one morning, Ethan crawled into bed with us and he was visibly distraught over a frightening dream he had. He was obviously incredibly upset. My son never dreams much or ever has nightmares that he ever reports—but this time was different. He described in his nightmare of seeing barracks-style military metal buildings that were very large, in which he saw people on fire and burning. One fellow, in particular, he saw with the flames shooting up all around him and over the top of him and Ethan said to me, "Mom, he was not a happy camper."

This dream seemed to be all too real to him. Well I calmed him down and got him off to school that morning and I was a little concerned about the unusual dream he had. In fact, we try hard to steer Ethan from movies, software, toys, and books that would lead him to have bad dreams.

Here is Ethan's version of what he dreamed or saw that morning:
I had this dream and in the dream I was in this diner and I ate breakfast in there it was a happy cheery place. There were tons of people in there eating breakfast it was in the morning and it was light out on a summer morning. Then, all of a sudden, I was in the car we were driving by this long building that was extremely long and that went on forever. It was like one of those metal army half-circle steel army buildings. And it had this guard at the front door.

The door was cement and you could see these flames seeping out the concrete door. Then all of a sudden, I was standing at the door of the diner, I had this metal or wood cross around my neck and I saw these two girls sitting at a table and it looked like the place was being lit by a fireplace and tables were turned over and chairs were broken apart. The place was a wreck but the table that the girls were sitting at was perfectly fine.

At that point, I ripped off my cross necklace clutching it in my hand I looked around the corner where the light was coming from and I saw the metal building coming in the side of diner as if it was in the diner and the flames that were shooting up from the ground touched the top of the metal building which was about 7 feet and I saw a person flailing around and banging the side of the building and he was in the metal building on fire—he looked like he was made out of fire and he was covered with fire at that point I stepped back out of the doorway and looked through the window, through one side of the pane the girls were looking at each and through the lower part of a different pane they were looking at me and I looked back and forth wondering how they could be different in two different panes in the same window. Then I dropped the cross in the doorway and saw myself running away and I woke up terrified

Later that morning, after dropping Ethan to school, I came home to read my morning devotional from a Christian book. This particular book speaks on the importance of the decisions made in this life to our eternal outcomes. The author felt that the Holy Spirit inspired the use of parables in this book, similar to how Jesus often spoke in parables.

As I was reading, I got to a part where the author describes a "parable" version of hell *as large metal, military barracks-style buildings in which people were burning or on fire!* The author also described these buildings as being very huge in size and going on forever. Amazingly, this was exactly how Ethan described seeing them in his dream/vision. I was dumbfounded by this description. *I couldn't believe this was identical to how Ethan had just described his bad dream to me that same morning **before I had ever read this passage from the book.***

I had not read this section of the book beforehand, nor had Ethan read any of it at all. He was not aware at all that I was even reading the book. I never had a reason to tell him I was reading such a book. I was simply amazed by this.

Immediately after school that same day, I read to Ethan that section from the book. I read about the author's version of hell and the parable about the metal buildings with people on fire. Ethan said to me, "That was just exactly like my dream!"

Even more incredibly, we had made a visit later in the year to the Dayton Air Force Museum in Ohio and there were several metal military barracks-style buildings around the museum. Ethan told me the buildings looked just like the ones he saw in his dream earlier in the year. It was an eye-opening experience for both of us.

God's Position on the Occult:
Fairies, Witches, Spells, Charms, Wizards

I used to collect all these "fairy" things just because I thought it was kind of cute and harmless. My friends would buy me all this fairy-related stuff for gifts. One friend gave me a sweater with fairies that I wore many times and I never thought anything about it.

One time, I was downtown Indianapolis at a major chain bookstore and my eye caught the cover of a wiccan (witchcraft) magazine, and I was surprised to find that there actually was a magazine dedicated to the subject of wiccan. A quick scan of the cover of this magazine surprised me when I saw that it had fairies on it. I thought to myself that there must be some kind of a connection to the occult and fairies and my heart was checked about collecting all the fairy stuff. Can you imagine a dedicated Christian collecting things related to witchcraft? That would be outrageous. However, I did not actually do anything about this revelation until sometime later.

One Sunday morning, I could not find anything I wanted to wear to church and I put that fairy sweater of mine on. I was in the bathroom at home at the time, getting ready for church, and the Lord spoke to me and He said plainly and clearly in an audible voice, ***"Don't dress the way the heathens' dress."*** Well let me say first, I never, ever use the word "heathens" for any reason myself. I was completely shocked and I knew it was about the fairy shirt I was wearing because I had already felt checked in my spirit about fairies because of the cover on the wiccan magazine I had seen. Immediately, I disposed of that shirt and I threw all my other fairy stuff out as well. If you do the research online, you will find the direct pagan connection between fairies with wiccan and witchcraft.

At one of my church board meetings, I shared the frustration I felt when I look through my son's elementary book orders of new book choices available to children offered through their schools no less. Then I cringed at my son's schoolbook sale over the new books that I was selling to second, third, and fourth graders while volunteering. Topics such as witchcraft, the occult, and all sorts of dark subject matter are prolific.

I was further irritated when I signed up my son for our local library summer reading club for kids. To acquire toys and prizes, a certain number of books were to be read by the participants over the summer. So, we went to look through the juvenile section for books in my son's age group. I was further frustrated when I spent time and effort to find titles appropriate, only to discover that the shelves were full of dark titles for kids. I was amazed that there were so few titles available that did not have dark subject matter.

There is a dark preoccupation with sinister subject matter focused straight at the children. The orientation is to all things related to the occult and dark themed characters—fairies, witches, warlocks, wizards, vampires, pirates, monsters, and psychics. Horror themed books and horoscopes for kids are all available to them. You can find these themes in all media forms: online, books, software, video gaming, magazines, movies, advertising, television, music lyrics, theme parks, and even museum exhibitions, and it is all available to children. Educators use these dark themes to promote "reading" to children, all the while, also educating children about things derived from the occult and other dark themes.

Books for kids seem to not be worthwhile unless they are about dark subject matter, horror, or the irreverent. Subjects such as righteousness and goodness are just not being popularized as much by the mainstream secular markets. It is hard to tell the good guys from the bad guys, because even the heroes in the current stories can take the role of a wizard or a vampire and they have some measure of the darkness which is glorified.

In our library summer reading club program with something like 20,000 local kids participating, multiple companies donate funding and slick brochures are produced and then several books are promoted for summer reading. Books highlighted for children to read over the summer focused on witches, fairies, wizards, and enchantresses.

It is all innocent fun and we are just trying to promote reading—don't be so prudish, you may say…

Well when did such dark material creep under our detection? In our public library, under Christian book titles for children you will find total 757 titles. When you search the topic heading *wizard* you will find 692 titles. Search *witches* and you find 1,200 titles, search *horror* and you will discover 3,521 titles, and 100 titles will be found under the heading *witchcraft* alone. I even ran across a book for kids on how to have a young witch sleepover party. Some of the titles are much darker and pervasive—describing chants, spells, sorcery, and divinations that children can learn to do.

Let's see what the Bible says: **Deuteronomy 18:9-13** is about detestable practices: *When thou art come into the land which the LORD thy God giveth thee, thou shalt not learn to do after the abominations of those nations. There shall not be found among you any one that maketh his son or his daughter to pass through the fire, or that useth divination, or an observer of times, or an enchanter, or a witch. Or a charmer, or a consulter with familiar spirits, or a wizard, or a necromancer. For all that do these things are an abomination unto the LORD: and because of these abominations the LORD thy God doth drive them out from before thee. Thou shalt be perfect with the LORD thy God.*

Did you read that verse? This is the Holy Word of God and you might need to read it again. I think the Bible is clear about God's position here on these matters.

So we have our children sliding down a slippery slope which is getting steeper and steeper—and no one seems to be paying attention. It is just kid stuff and it's all in good clean fun—or is it? I know that witches have been a subject matter for kids for many years, but the books out there for kids are much, much darker then they have ever been. Check it out for yourself. I think you will be surprised if you have not taken notice of this purposefully dark shift aimed at our children. I do not know what the answer is—but I believe it is a matter of serious prayer. Our children's very innocence is at stake. The enemy has found an easy entrance into the back doors or our safe havens and homes.

Matthew 18:6 says: *But whoso shall offend one of these little ones which believe in me, it were better for him that a millstone were hanged about his neck, and that he were drowned in the depth of the sea.*

One of the most current hailed characters in the history of children's literature I believe directly insults and blaspheme God. And, why not? God hates wizards and abhors the occult. God hates leading children astray and aiding and leading them to sin and toward evil. This famous character has a lightning bolt on his forehead and uses the name "Potter." When the Bible speaks of God, "lightning" is often associated with Him as in the following verses. The same holds true for God being described in the Bible as the great

"Potter." Now imagine, if you will, how unhappy God is that children are being filled with subject matter that glorifies and promotes the occult, witchcraft, and wizards.

God as the Lightning:

Exodus 19:16-17: *And it came to pass on the third day in the morning, that there were **thunders and lightnings**, and a thick cloud upon the mount, and the voice of the trumpet exceeding loud; so that all the people that was in the camp trembled. And Moses brought forth the people out of the camp to meet with God; and they stood at the nether part of the mount.*

Job 37:3: *He directeth it under the whole heaven, and **his lightning** unto the ends of the earth.*

Psalms 77:18: *The **voice of thy thunder** was in the heaven: the **lightnings** lightened the world: the earth trembled and shook.*

And here in particular Jesus talks about how God dealt with Satan:

Luke 10:18: *And he said unto them, I beheld Satan as **lightning** fall from heaven.*

God as the Potter:

Psalms 2:9: *Thou shalt break them with a rod of iron; thou shalt dash them in pieces like a **potter's vessel.***

Isaiah 29:16: *Surely your turning of things upside down shall be esteemed **as the potter's clay**: for shall the work say of him that made it, He made me not? Or shall the thing framed say of him that framed it, He had no understanding?*

Romans 9:21: *Hath not the **potter power over the clay**, of the same lump to make one vessel unto honor, and another unto dishonor?*

Some other comments in the Bible about God's hatred for witchcraft and sorcery:

2 Chronicles 33:6: *And he caused his children to pass through the fire in the valley of the son of Hinnom: also he observed times, and used enchantments, and used witchcraft, and dealt with a familiar spirit, and with wizards: he wrought much evil in the sight of the LORD, to provoke him to anger.*

Micah 5:12: *And I will cut off witchcrafts out of thine hand; and thou shalt have no more soothsayers:*

Galatians 5:19-21: *Now the works of the flesh are manifest, which are these; Adultery, fornication, uncleanness, lasciviousness, Idolatry, **witchcraft**, hatred, variance, emulations, wrath, strife, seditions, heresies, Envying, murders, drunkenness, revellings, and such like: **of the which I tell you before, as I have also told you in time past, that they which do such things shall not inherit the kingdom of God.***

Perhaps a good rule to go by for deciding what materials or programs you and your children can feel comfortable with can come from the Lord's Prayer and **Matthew 6:10:** *Thy kingdom come, Thy will be done in earth, as it is in Heaven.* If you can see yourself watching a TV show or reading a particular book in Heaven or at church, then it probably is safe. If you cannot imagine hearing a particular song in Heaven or playing a specific game at church is it right for you, now? You may say, "Wow, this is totally crazy and impossible." Here is the challenge…if you think you want to spend eternity in Heaven (and I hope you do), then why is it not practical to avoid the kind of materials you know you should not be exposed to right now?

The world's fascination with the occult is its admission that people are drawn to that sense that there is something more than the temporal world in front of us. If only people could see that it is God who is the source of all the things they are longing and looking for in their souls. People sense there is more, but sadly, they are being pulled to the wrong, poor substitute for God in the occult. Satan can only pervert

God's creation and only God can create anything. Turn to God in Who you can have all your spiritual longings met.

Psalms 68:1

While my family went to a local electronics store, I decided to visit a local Christian bookstore just to look around while they shopped nearby. I found a book that looked interesting. I decided to find a chair and to sit and I flipped through the book and checked different sections while I sat there and waited for the others to shop.

As I browsed through this one book, I came across the passage **Psalms 68:1** and it read: *To the chief Musician, A Psalm or Song of David.* ***"Let God arise."*** Well as I sat there reading this particular passage out of the Psalms, I could not help but to be amazed at the music that was piped in and playing overhead as I read. The song played with lyrics that **continuously repeated** ***"Let God Arise"***—the identical phrase of the Bible verse I just happened to be reading. Was this was just another one of many incredible coincidences?

Psalms 68:1: ***Let God arise*** *let his enemies be scattered: let them also that hate him flee before him.*

Romans 7:20-23

One remarkable morning something startling happened. I was reading a book all about God and the particular section I was reading was all about the Apostle Paul's struggle with sin and **Romans 7:20-23** was quoted.

Romans 7:20-23: *Now if I do that I would not, it is no more I that do it, but sin that dwelleth in me. I find then a law, that, when I would do good, evil is present with me. For I delight in the law of God after the inward man: But I see another law in my members, warring against the law of my mind, and bringing me into captivity to the law of sin which is in my members.*

I decided then in the next moment to read out of my Bible, I opened it up randomly and looked down, and my eyes fell exactly on **Romans 7:20-23**! I had been reading the exact verses in the other book just prior to opening the Bible. It was also amazing, but I had just been talking to God in prayer earlier how glad I was to think that this matter of struggling with sin was in God's hand once He takes over. Now how does He do these things? I have to say that I am stunned when this happens. I cannot imagine how this occurs—it is overwhelming, yet it happens to me frequently. Nevertheless, as I said, I have experienced it many, many times and it is miraculous. The Bible is truly alive and the Holy Spirit is truly at work.

One day I was traveling in my car home alone after taking my son to school and all the time talking aloud to God. During that time, I quoted this verse **1 Corinthians 2:9:** *But as it is written, Eye hath not seen, nor ear heard, neither have entered into the heart of man, the things which God hath prepared for them that love him.*

As soon as I arrived home, I began to prepare for my weekly Bible study—and I came on to this same verse, right after I had quoted it to God in the car. I had no idea I would randomly come to this verse after referring to it in my prayer just earlier.

Chapter Eighteen—Gazing on God

Gazing on God*

Early one morning, while driving back from my son's school, I was having my usual discussion with God and I sincerely requested of Him in these words exactly that, ***I might forever be with the Lord and to gaze on him forever.*** Just a little bit after that, I arrived home and while eating some breakfast, I was doing my devotions and reading the book, *"The Importance of Being Foolish—How to Think Like Jesus,"* authored by Brennan Manning (one of my personal favorite writers), and very soon came upon this verse he sites in the book **Psalms 27:4** in which the author of the verse talks about dwelling in the house of the Lord all the days of his life and to gaze upon the beauty of the Lord.

I was a little stunned to say the least, given that I had just an hour before asked that *I might forever be with the Lord and to gaze on Him forever*. **Psalms 27:4** essentially says the same thing.

If you think about our relationship to God from the stand point that God created us for Himself and if our being and existence comes from Him, then why should we not want to give Him our time, consideration, and friendship? Whenever I have visited the youth for my church outreach Juvenile Center ministry, I ask them a question to get them to think about who they are in relation to God. I ask them if they were God and they had created humans—how would they feel if the humans they created did not care about them or even give them the time of day. They always react with an attitude of annoyance that they should be ignored by the humans they created. Then I ask them how they are any different when they themselves ignore God? We owe everything to God—our being, salvation, and hopefully our future with Him. Why then do we squeeze out so little time for God? Why do we only fit Him into the cracks and crevices of our lives?

The things of the world used to hold me under its spell—pursuing position, security through finances, and satisfaction through the things around me. Then I found that the world and people are temporal, untrustworthy, unpredictable, and unreliable. These disappointments in the world led me to realize only God is completely reliable, trustworthy, infinite, and consistently the same: yesterday, today, and tomorrow. The securest place we can ever be is safe in His loving arms for all eternity. So logically, if we make no time for God in this life, how do we honestly expect that God will believe that when this temporal life we are leading is over that suddenly we will want to give Him all our time for an eternity?

The Bible makes it clear that God will assume that we do not want to spend time with Him in eternity if we do not devote our lives to Him in this world. I do not believe that this means looking for every church activity to sign up for either. I truly believe that God wants the "first fruits" of our time and that means a close personal friendship with Him. Sometimes, too many church activities can even distract us from developing a relationship with God. We need to weigh these things out and choose to spend time getting to know God better through prayer and reading His Word on our own before we fill our extra time with church activities.

Jesus was asked one time what was the most important commandment (of the Ten Commandments that God gave Moses) and Jesus said the first most important commandment is to love the Lord your God with all your soul, heart, strength, and mind. Does your life reflect this commandment? After lots of contemplation, I have discerned that real treasure does not lie in pursuing the temporal things of this life or even the great things we read about Heaven in the Bible—but being near God Himself is where our true treasure exists.

*I just want to comment that one time when I was editing this same section a while later for this book, I was amazed again by what had happened to me and **immediately after working on this section,** I received a heart-warming email from a friend. She spoke these words in her email: "We get to behold our LORD and GAZE ON HIS GLORIOUS MAGNIFICENCE forever!" These were the words she capped in her email. I was amazed that my friend had worded her email to me like this right after I was going over this particular section. God never ceases to amaze.*

I want to add something to this section that much later, perhaps a year later I was once again pleading my case to God that I knew that I was no one special but that I thought spending time near God for eternity must be wonderful. Now immediately following my prayer, I had taken to reading a book written by Charles Spurgeon, a well-known evangelist. Here is the amazing thing that I read. Spurgeon said that when we have certain spiritual desires that God actually puts these longings in our hearts because it is how He plans to bless us and that He plants desires there of what He plans to do for us. Spurgeon goes on to say that if God places such spiritual desires (the key here is the spiritual desires) in our heart that He will not disappoint us.

Psalms 37:4: *Delight thyself also in the LORD: and he shall give thee the desires of thine heart.*

Deep Calling Unto Deep

I woke up one morning and first heard the Lord saying to me: ***"Deep calling unto deep."*** I had never heard this phrase before in my life then and it was completely unfamiliar to me. After hearing this phrase, I had to look to see if, and where, it might be in the Bible. Then yes, I found it in the Bible—verse **Psalms 42:7.** I also had no clue this phrase could be found in the Bible. Here is the entire section that phrase actually comes from written by David:

Psalms 42:1-11: *As the hart panteth after the water brooks, so panteth my soul after thee, O God. My soul thirsteth for God, for the living God: when shall I come and appear before God? My tears have been my meat day and night, while they continually say unto me, Where is thy God? When I remember these things, I pour out my soul in me: for I had gone with the multitude, I went with them to the house of God, with the voice of joy and praise, with a multitude that kept holyday. Why art thou cast down, O my soul? And why art thou disquieted in me? Hope thou in God: for I shall yet praise him for the help of his countenance. O my God, my soul is cast down within me: therefore will I remember thee from the land of Jordan, and of the Hermonites, from the hill Mizar. DEEP CALLETH UNTO DEEP at the noise of thy waterspouts: all thy waves and thy billows are gone over me. Yet the LORD will command his lovingkindness in the day time, and in the night his song shall be with me, and my prayer unto the God of my life. I will say unto God my rock, why hast thou forgotten me? why go I mourning because of the oppression of the enemy? As with a sword in my bones, mine enemies reproach me; while they say daily unto me, Where is thy God? Why art thou cast down, O my soul? and why art thou disquieted within me? hope thou in God: for I shall yet praise him, who is the health of my countenance, and my God.*

Sometimes those around us see us going through a difficult patch of life and make us feel like, "Where is that God she talks about all the time?" No matter what life throws at us, we can be certain that *God is near.* And, there is nothing going on that is not part of His perfect will. Because this life is temporal, true followers of Christ are being prepared to be with God for eternity and part of growing towards God in this life will include many character-building experiences. I have never seen much character ever built in times of plenty and when things are going the way we want them going. We grow when we learn about humility towards God, helpless dependence on God and, ultimately grasp the importance of child-like faith.

Charles Spurgeon writes about the meaning of **"Deep calling unto deep"** in this section of the Bible almost like the perfect storm of wave upon wave of troubles crashing down on the helpless person. Sometimes God allows such struggles two-fold in our lives that we can feel them on the outside as they are happening to us to how we feel them on the inside producing a painful inner struggle. Through the perfect storm, God is present. When God's children experience this kind of intense experience, God simultaneously delivers the grace in measure equal to the suffering He allows in His perfect will.

What a testimony to the individual experiencing such extremes and what a testimony to those who witness this happening. How can someone in the depths of the deep demonstrate such displays of inner peace? David describes his own life in this verse and his life was riddled with struggles. So was this the case for Daniel and the Apostle Paul. Only God can deliver that amazing peace that surpasses all understanding in the midst of the perfect storm you are going through.

Will the Christian that moves close to God be able to avoid troubles? Probably not in this life. Troubles will come—but God delivers His grace incrementally to the troubles you suffer. Lean on Him in your darkest hour and He will deliver the kind of peace *that can never be found* through the world.

Hosea and Gomer

If you read the story of the prophet Hosea in the book Hosea, you will see that God told him to go marry a prostitute and help her to become a faithful wife. Even after Hosea marries Gomer, she strays to other lovers. God tells Hosea that His people are like the prostitute Gomer and that He will cause them to leave their lovers and return to Him. God instructs Hosea to take his money, buy Gomer back, spare no expense, and to bring her home again. This story represented the troubles God had with His people. This is an amazing story of God's touching love for His people and willingness to forgive their sins and bring them back to Himself.

I had never heard this particular Bible story before and at the time, I was reading a book about God and I came to an entire section that tells of the story between Hosea and Gomer.

Hosea 2:6: *Therefore, behold, I will hedge up thy way with thorns, and make a wall, that she shall not find her paths.*

Now imagine this, I had never heard this Bible story before. I read about it one night and the next morning when I picked up my email, my devotional email comes in and it is all about Hosea, Gomer, and **Hosea 2:6**.

So what are your other "lovers" that distract you from God?

God's Incredible Special Order

On vacation my family was busy watching a DVD they had gotten for Christmas and I was in the same room reading a book by the famous English evangelist Charles Spurgeon titled, *"A Passion for Holiness in a Believer's Life."*

I came to a whole section of the book written all about this particular verse: **Psalms: 119:133:** *Order my steps in thy word: and let not any iniquity have dominion over me.* The entire section I was reading was about how God *orders* our steps and I was reading about Spurgeon's discussion regarding this verse. It is safe to say that the entire section was about *"God's order for our lives."* At one point, Spurgeon writes: "**Order** thy steps in thy word. Put me under **orders**, keep me under **orders**, and never let me escape Your **orders**." This whole section was focused on God's order for our lives.

As I said before while reading this section, my family was in the same room engrossed in an animated movie and all of a sudden, one of the characters in the movie starts talking about some sort of "**order**." Then, as I was reading all about how our steps are being **ordered** by God—one of the characters in the movie playing nearby me says three times, **"Special Order, Special Order, Special Order."** I was struck with amazement and once again, I hardly thought this was some wild coincidence, but a display of God's incredible timing and **ordering** of the steps of my life.

When you talk about our steps ordered by God, you will agree that you can see how I wonder about these amazing events being more than just a lot of uncanny coincidences. Like the time I was traveling home in the car on a long trip and I was engrossed in a book by the historic evangelist Charles Spurgeon called *"A Passion for Holiness in a Believer's Life."* My husband, who was driving the car, had no clue what I was reading as he sat next to me. I came to this section in the book where Spurgeon writes: *"But I think that until you die, you will have some evil to struggle with. As long as you are in this body, **there will be*** *enough tinder for one of the devil's sparks to set it afire. You will have need to* **keep on damping it and every moment** *be on the watchtower, even till you cross the Jordan."* Well as I am reading this paragraph, my husband is on the cell phone with his Father at the same time and Steve asks him **whether the wood was too damp to burn?** I looked over at my husband on the phone wondering what is causing him to say this, with the content that is nearly identical to what I am reading. So, after Steve hangs up, I ask him if he did indeed just ask his Father about trying to burn damp wood or maybe I had just heard wrong. He confirmed that he asked his Dad about some wood in our yard to burn in his Dad's fireplace and if it was too damp and green to burn.

Another time I was at church for dinner and a good friend was sitting next to me at the table. I had on my mind something wonderful God had done for me. I thought to myself, *"God had my back!"* At the exact moment I had this thought, my friend sitting next to me at the table, out of the blue, immediately started talking to me about her Husband's "back." I am thinking to myself that this is a very strange thing. I had to laugh it was just too funny.

I have to describe yet another time something happened that required God's precision timing. I was reading a book about God and the content was about how God is always watching over us even in the *"middle of the night."* No real exciting thing, except my son had a children's CD playing in the room and the narrator on the CD said the words *"middle of the night"* exactly as I read the same words in my book. It was extraordinary. Let me add, that when this happens, I cannot ignore it because it is incredibly hard to miss.

This is funny, but true. We were driving to Florida over one recent spring break, and we drove past an antique car on the road with an old fashioned **rumble** seat in the back—which my husband happened to notice and commented on. I was reading the verse **Isaiah 4:5** in the Bible about the throne of God and just as I read this copy: *from the throne came flashes of lightning,* **rumblings** *and peals of thunder*—from the backseat of the car, my son yelled out the word "RUMBLE" just exactly as I was reading the word **"rumblings"** in this verse—in perfect synchronization. There was no way that my son knew at the time that I was reading that verse and that he would say RUMBLE—when I read the word RUMBLINGS exactly. You know, I just have to laugh at the incredible humor and timing of God.

Yet another time, my son and I were eating dinner at a restaurant just the two of us. He was wearing headphones plugged into his iPod™ and he was listening to an audio Bible. I was saying to Ethan the words, *"I had to give God the credit."* At that moment, Ethan's eyes became like two silver dollars and he told me that as I was saying, *"Give God the Credit"* that the narrator he was listening to on his iPod™ said the same words *"give God the credit"* right as I said it.

While I was reading the wonderful book by Brennan Manning, one of my favorite writers, titled, *"The Relentless Tenderness of Jesus"* (this is an awesome read by the way)—well anyway, I was reading away and I was sitting in the car waiting and killing time. Ethan had a music CD playing. Now what happened next was crazy. I mean crazy! I came to the word "WHISPER" in the book and here is the craziest thing— at the moment I read the word WHISPER—the singer on the CD sang the words "You WHISPER." And, I heard the word "WHISPER" on the CD at the same time I read it.

I recall another time I was reading the Bible in the car while my son was listening to his music CD. When I came to the word "TWIST" in the verse, the singer on the CD sang the word "TWIST" exactly as I read it. Now how common is the word twist and with what precision does it take to line up my reading of the word TWIST in the Bible to a someone singing the word TWIST simultaneously? The verse I read was **Deuteronomy 16:19**.

Now one of the reasons I am writing about all these precision coincidences is for me to show the amazing way God orchestrates our lives with His perfect order and exactness. Wouldn't we all be incredibly more relaxed, once we give God our lives to realize that He orders our steps—everyday, every hour, every minute, every second? It has been a huge relief for me to realize how precisely God actually orchestrates our lives.

Bible Book Ends

In April of 2008, I was leading a Bible Study and I asked everyone there that if they were ever lacking in perspective about life *to read the first two and the last two chapters of the Bible.* **Genesis 1-2** and **Revelation 21-22** are scenes of God's perfection. **Genesis 3** through **Revelation 20** are bookends between an imperfect sin-filled world.

Then incredibly, I went home that night following my Bible Study and once again, I decided to check my day's email messages. Up popped my daily devotional email, and I was amazed that the devotion cited the same information I had used on a computer presentation slide for the Bible study earlier *that same day* about the *first two and last two chapters* of the Bible and the sin in between and the perfection at the beginning and end in the Bible. It was truly astounding. And, just what are the odds that I should talk about this concept to consider the first two chapters of Genesis and the last two chapters of Revelations and both referring to God's perfect worlds—only to open an email devotion with that exact concept the same day. I had no foreknowledge that my email devotion that night would match the discussion I had with my Bible Study group to that precise detail. God is amazing!

You might note that in an entire average Bible, there are as many as 1,189 chapters. So, what are the chances that these four exact chapters could be highlighted in my Bible Study computer slide and then again in an email devotion in the same evening with the same identical unique message? I find this to be simply astounding.

Moses and Aaron

Moses and his brother Aaron were assigned by God to lead the Israelites out of Egypt and on their way in the desert wilderness. Their goal was to make it to the Promised Land. Along the way though, the Israelites would complain about many things. One day the people were unhappy with Moses and Aaron leading them. The people challenged their authority and God was furious with the people for challenging His decision for Moses and Aaron to lead them. Now the three heading up the opposition of Moses and Aaron were Korah, Dathan, and Abiram. (You can read what happened to them in **Numbers 16:1-33** below.)

I was reading **"Numbers 16:1-33"** as my morning Bible study one day. Then I decided to spend time praying and sometimes when I pray, I also read out of my Bible. This was one of those days and I decided to read from the book of **Psalms.** *I randomly opened the Bible and turned to "Psalms 106:16-18 first. Amazingly, I came upon the one section of Psalms that spoke of the same incident in the Bible about Moses and Aaron that I had just read a few minutes earlier in Numbers. Incredibly, by random chance, I turned to the one reference elsewhere in the Bible about the same incident I had just read in Numbers (in fact, I did not even know that there was a reference to this particular story elsewhere in the Bible). I had no clue that this would happen.*

You can see the two sections here below—first the one I read in my morning Bible study and second the verse I randomly opened to in the Bible while praying that same morning:

What I read about in my personal Bible study one morning:

Numbers 16:1-33: *Now Korah, the son of Izhar, the son of Kohath, the son of Levi, and Dathan and Abiram, the sons of Eliab, and On, the son of Peleth, sons of Reuben, took men: And they rose up before Moses, with certain of the children of Israel, two hundred and fifty princes of the assembly, famous in the congregation, men of renown: And they gathered themselves together against Moses and against Aaron, and said unto them, Ye take too much upon you, seeing all the congregation are holy, every one of them, and the LORD is among them: wherefore then lift ye up yourselves above the congregation of the LORD? And when Moses heard it, he fell upon his face: And he spake unto Korah and unto all his company, saying, Even tomorrow the LORD will shew who are his, and who is holy; and will cause him to come near unto him: even him whom he hath chosen will he cause to come near unto him. This do; Take you censers, Korah, and all his company; And put fire therein, and put incense in them before the LORD tomorrow: and it shall be that the man whom the LORD doth choose, he shall be holy: ye take too much upon you, ye sons of Levi. And Moses said unto Korah, Hear, I pray you, ye sons of Levi: Seemeth it but a small thing unto you, that the God of Israel hath separated you from the congregation of Israel, to bring* *you near to himself to do the service of the tabernacle of the LORD, and to stand before the congregation to minister unto them? And he hath brought thee near to him and all thy brethren the sons of Levi with thee: and seek ye the priesthood also? For which cause both thou and all thy company are gathered together against the LORD: and what is Aaron that ye murmur against him? And Moses sent to call Dathan and Abiram, the sons of Eliab: which said, We will not come up: Is it a small thing that thou hast brought us up out of a land that floweth with milk and honey, to kill us in the wilderness, except thou make thyself altogether a prince over us? Moreover thou hast not brought us into a land that floweth with milk and honey, or given us inheritance of fields and vineyards: wilt thou put out the eyes of these men? We will not come up. And Moses was very wroth, and said unto the LORD, Respect not thou their offering: I have not taken one ass from them, neither have I hurt one of them. And Moses said unto Korah, Be thou and all thy company before the LORD, thou, and they, and Aaron, tomorrow: And take every man his censer, and put incense in them, and bring ye before the LORD every man his censer, two hundred and fifty censers; thou also, and Aaron, each of you his censer. And they took every man his censer, and put fire in them, and laid incense thereon, and stood in the door of the tabernacle of the congregation with Moses and Aaron. And Korah gathered the entire congregation against them unto the door of the tabernacle of the congregation: and the glory of the LORD appeared unto the entire congregation. And the LORD spake unto Moses and unto Aaron, saying, Separate yourselves from among this congregation, that I may consume them in a moment. And they fell upon their faces, and said, O God, the God of the spirits of all flesh, shall one man sin, and wilt thou be worth with all the congregation? And the LORD spake unto Moses, saying, Speak unto the congregation, saying, Get you up from about the tabernacle of Korah, Dathan, and Abiram. And Moses rose up and went unto Dathan and Abiram; and the elders of Israel followed him. And he spake unto the congregation, saying, Depart, I pray you, from the tents of these wicked men, and touch nothing of theirs, lest ye be consumed in all their sins. So they gat up from the tabernacle of Korah, Dathan, and Abiram, on every side: and Dathan and Abiram came out, and stood in the door of their tents, and their wives, and their sons, and their little children. And Moses said, Hereby ye shall know that the LORD hath sent me to do all these works; for I have not done them of mine own mind. If these men die the common death of all men, or if they be visited after the visitation of all men; then the LORD hath not sent me. But if the LORD make a new thing, and the earth open her mouth, and swallow them up, with all that appertain unto them, and they go down quick into the pit; then ye shall understand that these men have provoked the LORD. And it came to pass, as he had made an end of speaking all these words, that the ground clave asunder that was under them: And the earth opened her mouth, and swallowed them up, and their houses, and all the men that appertained unto Korah, and all their goods. They, and all that appertained to them, went down alive into the pit, and the earth closed upon them: and they perished from among the congregation.*

What I *first* opened to in the Bible *randomly that same morning* later while I was praying:

Psalms 106:16-18: *They envied Moses also in the camp, and Aaron the saint of the LORD. The earth opened and swallowed up Dathan and covered the company of Abiram. And a fire was kindled in their company; the flame burned up the wicked.*

Chapter Nineteen—Song of Solomon

Song of Solomon

For some reason one day, without any explanation, of all the books in the Old Testament I decided to focus on the Song of Solomon. Considering I had concentrated on reading the New Testament, it was highly unusual for me to suddenly be interested in the Old Testament.

After reading the Song of Solomon, I decided I wanted more insight on what I had read—so I began to look online and I came to a *"Devotional Commentary on the Song of Solomon"* that I also felt compelled to read. The day I printed out some of the Song of Solomon Devotional I had found online and when I came home, someone had the TV playing in the house and there was a minister talking about the Song of Solomon! I thought to myself, "Wow is that a confirmation that I should read the Song of Solomon study?"

The *"Devotional Commentary on the Song of Solomon"* intrigued me and the author tells a wonderful story of how the study came into existence. The author, Esher Shoshannah, a Holy Spirit-filled minister was asked to prepare a Bible study for his wife and some other ladies. He was not too crazy about the idea but was talked into it and he decided to do it on the Song of Solomon because he had several notes already prepared on that book.

Esher Shoshannah said that he would get up early in the morning to prepare for the Bible Study and the Holy Spirit revealed to him what the underlying meanings are of the story told in the Song of Solomon between the Bride and Solomon. Solomon in this Holy Book really represents Christ and the bride actually represents the Bride of Christ, the Church of Christ. Not unlike the way Christ spoke in parables and John Bunyan who wrote the classic *"Pilgrim's Progress"* in parables, so is the Song of Solomon Devotional. Many of the messages to us, from God, through the Bible are written as parables and stories.

Because the Holy Spirit revealed insight and meanings freely to Esher Shoshannah, the *"Devotional Commentary on the Song of Solomon"* is to never be sold. Acquire this study free by downloading the E-book at http://songofsolomondevotional.com. To learn more about the wonderful background behind this beautiful study, please visit http://songofsolomondevotional.com/history.php.

I read through the Song of Solomon study twice and I spent a lot of time with it the first time. The devotion was so life-changing that I decided to share the study with a group of ladies in a special Bible study I started and I was able to read through it again and I enjoyed it even more the second time. I know now that the Holy Spirit miraculously led me to experience this amazing book of the Bible and this supernaturally inspired devotional study because I was focused on the New Testament at the time and there was no rhyme or reason at all for me to want to read the Song of Solomon out-of-the-blue. As I read this study, I encountered many miraculous events and I fell in love with and saw Christ in a whole new way I had never before experienced.

After leading a group of ladies through this Devotional Study, I shared the book with others I know the Lord wanted this study to go to and also bless. Now two of the ladies in my study have taken the book to their churches for Bible studies and one study I know of that took place at my church's sister church was truly a blessing to those who experienced it.

I highly recommend that you also obtain a free copy of this amazing Devotional Study and take time to read the Song of Solomon and you will learn of the intense love Jesus has for you. In the following section, I will attempt to share and describe the miraculous things that accompanied my reading of this beautiful and Holy Spirit-filled study of the Song of Solomon.

Searching for Fulfillment

I was alone in the car and talking away to God one evening. I said to Him that I realized that after focusing on pursuing career, marriage, parenting, and material things that nothing but God really ultimately satisfies—all is vanities of vanities—everything is vanity. Moreover, I truly meant it when I said it. *Later that same night* I continued my reading in the *"Devotional Commentary on the Song of Solomon,"* just after I had confessed to God that pursuing everything but God left me empty without Him. This is the copy I read only about an hour later:

"In the past I searched for fulfillment in worldly philosophies, material things, friends, activities, family, and position, but alas they all failed me and left me in a desperate condition. You came where I was and gently picked me up and gave me life from the tree of Calvary"—"A Devotional Commentary of the Song of Solomon"

It was just unbelievable that I had these exact thoughts about one hour before I read the same thing in the devotional study. And no, I had no idea I would be reading this section. This amazed me.

Finding Rest in the Lord

God never ceases to amaze me. While reading the *"Devotional Commentary on the Song of Solomon"* study I was also reading a book during the same timeframe about walking closer with God. Now here is the strange thing that happened. Wow! I was reading from both books in the same day and the sections I came to, in both, addressed the exact same subject/topic. Each simultaneously cited the same exact verses:

Matthew 11:28-30: *Come unto me, all ye that labor and are heavy laden, and I will give you rest. Take my yoke upon you, and learn of me; for I am meek and lowly in heart: and ye shall find rest unto your souls. For my yoke is easy, and my burden is light.*

Both sections were speaking of resting in Christ and resist from doing too many church activities and not actually spending enough time with Christ*. They also spoke on putting all your worries on Him. Here is what went through my mind: WOW! HOW IS IT THAT I AM READING TWO DIFFERENT THINGS AND SIMULTANEOUSLY I READ THE SAME MESSAGE IN BOTH BOOKS AT THE SAME TIME QUOTING THE SAME VERSES? At the time, my thoughts were that these miraculous things never get old and I felt that I must have been reading the right thing for the two distinctly different books I had chosen to read to line up so perfectly with *the same message, being read at the same time.*

*Just a note about the section above: when I was going back over this section to edit it, I added the word "actually" to this sentence: resist from doing too many church activities and **NOT ACTUALLY SPENDING ENOUGH TIME WITH CHRIST.** *I have to tell you that as I was working on this the TV was playing in the background and as I inserted the word "actually" the TV news anchor said,* **"NOT SPENDING ENOUGH TIME."** *I sat back stunned in my chair for quite awhile.*

Taste That I Am Sweet

I was alone and driving in my car on the way to pick up my son at school and without warning, I heard the Lord simply say to me audibly these words:

"Taste that I am sweet."

Right after that experience (again, I had no foreknowledge of what I would read in this section), this is the section that I came to read in the *"Devotional Commentary on the Song of Solomon"*:

Song of Solomon 2:3: *As the apple tree among the trees of the wood, so is my beloved among the sons. I sat down under his shadow with great delight,* ***and his fruit was sweet to my taste.***

The Bride compares her Beloved to a tree in the forest that stands out above all others. There was a tree in the Garden of Eden that also stood out above all others, the tree of life in the middle of the Garden of Eden. Our forefathers did not take of that beautiful tree (Genesis 2:9). Glory to God, there was another tree that stood in the midst of a garden (John 19:18, 41), the tree of Calvary. Praise God for Calvary! What was a deadly poison to my Lord, became a sweet taste to me when I received the fruit from Calvary's tree!

"...I sat down under his shadow with great delight, and his fruit was sweet to my taste."

The bride so pleased His heart because she took time to sit under His shadow. She gave up other things to learn of Him and be changed by Him. As a believer she surrendered to "His shadow" and willingly placed herself under it. This is what two of John the Baptist's disciples did when they stood and watched Jesus. John the Baptist instructed them to "Behold the Lamb" and that is exactly what they did. Because of what John's followers observed they went to Jesus and "sat down under His shadow." These two disciples were changed men after that (John 1:35-43).

What was there about His shadow, which brought her great delight? She experienced His blessed abiding shelter protecting her (Psalms 91:1) and being hidden in His hand (Isaiah 49:2). His help lead her, and caused her to rejoice and sing (Psalms 63:7).

With joyous excitement she declares, "Lord, in my heart and spirit I sit next to You and I feel so unafraid and peaceful. O my loving Husband what utter delight You bring to the deep recesses of my heart. Nothing has ever satisfied me before, until I surrendered to Your loving, protecting, reassuring arms. The fruit from Your tree meets my every need, every minute of my life: the fruit of love, joy, peace, long-suffering, gentleness, goodness, faith, meekness, and self-control. It is sweet tasting! You have never given me fruit that has a bitter taste. I worship You, dear Lord Jesus, Get all the glory.

Astonishing, astounding—this was truly and undeniably, a miraculous encounter beyond-belief! I cannot begin to tell you how this experience affected me. Even as I edit this section for this book, I still find this to be a beautiful and glorious event that I will never forget. *To hear such sweet words audibly from the Lord and then to receive a confirmation of the words by the content of what I read next was overwhelming.*

I would especially like to note that at the time I was reading this section, I was actually going through many important changes in my commitment to spending more time reading my Bible, reading books about God, and prayer time. Therefore, in reality, *I had been spending more time under the Lord's shadow.*

My hope is that you will find encouragement from this and the other things I am reporting and that you will see how truly God desires intimacy with His followers. In addition, you will realize how by making Christ the Lord of your life and surrendering to Him, you will receive, in exchange, a wonderful everlasting relationship with the One who loves you, as no other ever will.

Psalms 34:8: *O taste and see that the LORD is good: blessed is the man that trusteth in him.*

Broad Shield

While going over the *"Devotional Commentary on the Song of Solomon"* for my Bible study, at the time a storm outside happened to be coming through the area. Because of the storm, I had turned on the TV weather news and at the same time, I was reading the section in the study specifically all about the ***Lord's shield of faith*** over us. I was stunned when suddenly the TV weatherman started to talk about a weather front coming in that he described as a **"BROAD SHIELD."** I am wondering to myself—just how many times does a weatherman ever use a term like that? It was so amazing that he used **"broad shield"** to describe the weather as I am reading a section of the book focused on one of the specific items of the armor of God—the **"shield."** Here is the section I was reading at the time:

The enemy would try to wear you down by the oppressive heat of the noon day. She followed the Lord and met with others in His flock. She found His shadow. The closer she drew to Him, the less effective were the weapons of the wicked one (Ephesians 6:16: In addition to all this, take up the shield of faith, with which you can extinguish all the flaming arrows of the evil one.). It is the "shield of faith" that stops all the fiery *missiles. A **shield** shadows you from the attack! Praise God for His shadow protecting against the fiery heat of the enemy's missiles!*

Little Foxes

One Sunday evening, a thought came into my mind and it was **"The little foxes spoil the vines."** At the time, I acknowledged that I recognized the verse from the Bible but I was not sure why it had come to mind.

I went on to help my son with his homework that night and I got him into bed. Then afterwards, I took time to read my *"Devotional Commentary on the Song of Solomon"* and I was stunned as I soon turned to a section that was all about **Song of Solomon 2:15** and how the little foxes spoil the vines. It was incredible—I had no foreknowledge that I would be reading all about this verse when I had thought of the very same verse earlier that same evening. Here is the verse I read later, that same night:

Song of Solomon 2:15: *Take us the foxes, the little foxes that spoil the vines: for our vines have tender grapes.*

This is the section from the *"Devotional Commentary on the Song of Solomon"*:

*Little foxes are known for their crafty, devious natures, hence the expression, "sly as a fox!" They love grapes and by nipping away at the tender shoots they can destroy whole vineyards. O the ugliness that little foxes bring into our lives. How it hurts the heart of the Lord Jesus Christ. He gave us everything necessary to keep our life lovely, pure and holy before Him (**1 Corinthians 7:1 and 2 Peter 1:3, 4**)! Then our sinful nature rises up and wants its way. This opens the door for a demonic little fox to come into our life and distract our vision of Him.*

*Is there a little fox in your life robbing you of the awareness of His consuming **"first love"** love for you and robbing Him of your once, all-consuming, **"first love"** love for Him? Is there an unconfessed sin in your walk: a habit, anger, bitterness, divorce, envy, fear, gossip, jealousy, lies, lust, impatience, worry, depression, discouragement, doubt, swearing or unforgiveness, etc.? Right now, confess it and repent of it so that the vine and grapes will not be destroyed. O do not let the tender grape and its wonderful fragrance be spoiled.!*

*How ready He is to forgive and restore you (**1 John 1:1-10**). The difficulty lies in that the foxes are "little!" Little foxes are cute and deceptively innocent but very, very dangerous! Those secular books you waste so much time over; the hours watching "just slightly bad" programs on TV, the decision to stay home when you really could go to be with other lilies at church; what harm could come from a "little" questionable program, pleasure, or amusement?*

The Pomegranates

Coincidence?—well I don't know, but one day my husband and son went to the grocery and proudly came back with a purchase they had never made before (or since). They found pomegranates and decided to get some to try. This fruit was new to my son. Now a day or so later to my shock—the section I came to in the *"Devotional Commentary on the Song of Solomon"* I had been reading was all about the symbolic meaning specifically about *pomegranates,* of all things. A big surprise for me that my son should purchase *pomegranates* right before I read about it and this is not something we ever purchase and have around our house as we did that particular week.

Here is the section I read all about pomegranates from the *"Devotional Commentary on the Song of Solomon"*:

Song of Solomon 6:7: *As a piece of a pomegranate are thy temples within thy locks.*

*Pomegranates are red and produce a red fruit juice. Red represents the blood of the Bridegroom. But now it appears on her temples instead of her lips, why? Let the word of God unlock the secret. Read **Exodus 28:33, 34, 39:24-26.** Pomegranates were embroidered upon the hem of the Levitical priest's robe. The* *priest represents sacrifice and worship to God, so also the Pomegranates. Pomegranates were carved on the Temple (**1 Kings 7:18:20**). The actual Temple in Jerusalem, built by Solomon, was the place designated by God where true sacrifice and worship was to take place. As a Blood-bought believer, her temples (the place of her thinking process) represent the area where they will chooses to sacrifice to God and worship Him. What she spoke of with her lips was constantly on her mind. And what was on her lips–praise and worship concerning her Beloved within the "holy place" behind the veil of her mind! The Holy Spirit declares in **1 Peter 2:5**: "You also, as living stones, are being built up a spiritual house, a holy priesthood, to offer up spiritual sacrifices acceptable to God through Jesus Christ." **1 Peter 2:9**: But you are a chosen people, a royal priesthood, a holy nation, a people belonging to God, that you may declare the praises of him who called you out of darkness into his wonderful light.*

Dorcas

One morning I was reading my Bible in **Acts 9:39** about how Christ's disciple Peter brought the woman, Dorcas, back to life and how her name means "gazelle." Well the section I read could be no more than four Bible verses long and she is certainly not a well-known character in the Bible. I simply had no rhyme or reason for reading this section and I just read it randomly. Then I was preparing for my Bible study for that week from the *"Devotional Commentary on the Song of Solomon"* and I was shocked when I came across this section of my Bible study within the same day:

*Gazelles are known for their quickness (**2 Samuel. 2:18**). The word "gazelle" in the Arabic means "affectionate." Also, the word for gazelle is the exact same Hebrew word translated "beauty." In **Isaiah 24:16**, it is used referring to giving "glory" to God. It is very instructive that the lady in **Acts 9:36**, who was raised from the dead by Peter was named Tabitha (also Dorcas). Tabitha is the Hebrew word and Dorcas is the Greek word for "gazelle"! This woman abounded with deeds of kindness, mercy, and charity. A spiritual gazelle is one who sees a need and quickly and quietly rushes to meet that need. How blessed she must have been (**Acts 20:35**)! What a beautiful Christian she was. Read her story found in **Acts 9:36-44**:*

Acts 9:36-44: *Now there was at Joppa a certain disciple named Tabitha, which by interpretation is called Dorcas: this woman was full of good works and alms deeds which she did. And it came to pass in those days, that she was sick, and died: whom when they had washed, they laid her in an upper chamber. And forasmuch as Lydda was nigh to Joppa, and the disciples had heard that Peter was there, they sent unto him two men, desiring him that he would not delay to come to them. Then Peter arose and went with them. When he was come, they brought him into the upper chamber: and all the widows stood by him weeping and shewing the coats and garments which Dorcas made, while she was with them. But Peter put them all forth, and kneeled down, and prayed; and turning him to the body said, Tabitha, arise. And she opened her eyes: and when she saw Peter, she sat up. And he gave her his hand, and lifted her up, and when he had called the saints and widows, presented her alive. And it was known throughout all Joppa; and many believed in the Lord. And it came to pass, that he tarried many days in Joppa with one Simon a tanner.*

Now really, what are the chances that I should read about this Bible character randomly in the same morning *(and remember it is only four verses out of the Bible, **Acts 9:36-44**)*. Then that I would read about her again in the same day of all the characters mentioned in the Bible—this just amazes me.

Garden of Our Hearts

As I was pulling out of my son's school parking lot, after dropping him off for the day, at that exact moment God gave me a picture in my mind—a vision. The only way I can describe what I saw was that when you read a book, often you have a picture in your mind of what you are reading and this is the closest way I have of describing what I saw. I did not actually see Jesus—but somehow I knew the vision was from Jesus. **I saw a seed, that I somehow knew had come from Jesus, being planted in the center of my heart. Then next coming up from the center of my heart, I saw a beautiful topiary full of red roses and it was growing up out of the center of my heart.** This all happened very quickly, but this was precisely what I saw. I believe the red roses symbolized the blood of Christ.

So later during that same day, I began to read my *"Devotional Commentary on the Song of Solomon"* right where I had left off and with complete shock, I opened to a large section in the study that talks about how

Christ plants a seed in our heart and from it a garden grows. And no, I had no foreknowledge that I would be reading about these things.

Now here is the section of the study I came to after the vision I received of Jesus' seed planted in my heart and from it seeing a beautiful red rose topiary growing up from the center of my heart:

*Dear Christian, what a beautiful compliment from Your Beloved to have your life be called a "garden" by Him! Did you know that God has His own garden, it is called "the garden of the Lord" in **Isaiah 51:3** and the Garden of Eden is called "the garden of God" in **Ezekiel 28:13**. God's wedding present to Adam and Eve was a garden in which He had already prepared for them. In that original garden a loving God placed all manner of wonderful things to be enjoyed through touch, taste, smell and vision. It was a place where God, longing for fellowship, could walk with man and share the wonders of His creation. It was the perfect setting for discussion, deliberation and devotion. God walked and talked with Adam in the garden. It was none other than Jesus Himself for He is the "Word of God" (**John 1:1**); He is "...all the fullness of the Godhead bodily" (**Colossians 2:9**). He is "...the express image of his (God's) person..." (**Hebrews 1:3**)!*

*Oh what infinite heart-wrenching pain Jesus must have felt when Adam and Eve chose another one to walk with after having committed spiritual adultery (**James 4:4**). **The garden of their heart** turned into hideous weeds of wickedness as did the actual physical garden. But, praise God, four thousand years later Jesus the Creator (**John 1:3, 10**) came back to earth to restore what sin had so corrupted. **He created a new spiritual garden for the heart of every believer. The Holy Spirit would plant it by applying the precious blood of Jesus to the spirit of man!** Man would become a new creation in Christ Jesus (**2 Corinthians 5:17**). **This wonderful spiritual heart garden would once again be a place where God and man could share intimately.***

A garden is where seeds are planted. Praise God for the powerful seed of the Word of God which was planted in the garden of our heart by the Holy Spirit (1 Peter 1:23)! Are you lovingly, with great expectation, meditating on your Bridegroom's Word? Are you expecting a great harvest from those seeds being planted into your heart? Here's how it is accomplished.

This garden of the heart is made spiritually beautiful through absolute surrender of the believer's will to the Lord (Romans 12:1). New and precious fruit begin to grow there for God and His children to enjoy. It will only happen as the Bride gives over the garden of her heart to the Father, the "husbandman" or "gardener" (John 15:1-11). With the Father having full rights to the garden of your heart, He instructs the Holy Spirit to break of the "fallow ground" (Jeremiah 4:3; Hosea 10:12). In grace He does for us what He had asked Israel to do! In this garden, through the power of the Holy Spirit, are planted glorious eternal seeds of His Word (Matthew 13:23)! O the blessed fruit that is produced: "love, joy, peace, long-suffering (patience), gentleness, goodness, faith, meekness, and temperance (self-control)" (Galatians 5:22-23)!

This was just phenomenal to me since I had no idea that I would be reading about ***"the garden of the heart"*** prior to the vision I was given and not until later in the *same day* did I read this section about *how the Lord plants a seed in our heart.* Moreover, the truth was that the Holy Spirit *was* changing my heart at the time also in a miraculous way.

Luke 8:15: *But that on the good ground are they, which in an honest and good heart, having heard the word, keep it, and bring forth fruit with patience.*

Hand-in-Hand in the Garden
The next morning, I was praying in the privacy of my bedroom and I said to Christ: ***"I saw myself walking together with Him hand-in-hand in a garden and He was showing me His favorite flowers."***

Really at the time, I was thinking—"Why am I praying this?"—and then I thought to myself, "Well, it sounds good." Then a stunning revelation came and *later that same day,* as I began my daily reading of the *"Devotional Commentary on the Song of Solomon"* study over my lunch, I was stunned as I came across a section that I did not know in advance I would be reading. ***The Bride in the story I was reading was*** *walking hand-in-hand in a garden together admiring the groom's favorite flowers.* I was completely floored. Here is the passage I read:

Song of Solomon 4:12: *A garden enclosed is my sister, my spouse; a spring shut up, a fountain sealed.*

*"...a spring shut up, a fountain sealed." Why is the spring of her heart shut up and the fountain of her heart sealed? At this point, her heart is for Him alone and no one else. He must receive the first fruits of surrender: love, worship, praise, and adoration flowing to His heart. The Jews were instructed to do that at harvest time (**Numbers 28:26; Nehemiah 10:34, 35**). When the garden of her heart is fully developed and the fruit and spices have come to harvest, then she invites her Beloved into her garden which she calls His garden in **Song of Solomon 4:16:***

Song of Solomon 4:16: *Awake, O north wind; and come, thou south; blow upon my garden, that the spices thereof may flow out. Let my beloved come into his garden, and eat his pleasant fruits.*

*After He has received His loving, first portion, then He allows others to be blessed from the garden of her heart and drink of the springs of living water (see **Song of Solomon 5:1**).*

Song of Solomon 5:1: *I am come into my garden, my sister, my spouse: I have gathered my myrrh with my spice; I have eaten my honeycomb with my honey; I have drunk my wine with my milk: eat, O friends; drink, yea, drink abundantly, O beloved.*

*But for now it is sealed, waiting for Him to come at the appropriate time to enjoy a heart filled with faith, filled with love and filled with the Holy Spirit. And when He opens it up, from the spring and fountain of her heart shall flow rivers of living water - refreshing, delightful waters of submission and obedience flowing back to His heart (**Ephesians 5:18-19**). As she listens to His quiet voice her heart pounds with love for Him. She questions, "Am I dreaming, or is this all for real? Can it be the Bridegroom of my heart, the God of the universe, has said all of this to me - to me, a nobody in the eyes of the world!" **He takes her by the hand and says, "Let's walk together in the garden for awhile, My love. And as we walk, I will show you just what I see inside of you that causes My heart to overflow in love." He gives her hand a gentle squeeze as they begin to walk. Beaming with joy He excitedly says, "Look how your garden is filled with My favorite fruits and flowers! They are so beautiful to Me My love." He stops and just takes in the joy of all the beauty of colors and the fragrances. "My love, look, look over there - you have these wonderful yellow Henna flowers in your garden.** Let's get a little closer." He picks a flower and puts it in her hair. "That flower is so beautiful, let me just step back and enjoy looking at you for a moment. I can't wait to share the flowers, fruit and spices of your heart with My friends (**Romans 8:29**)!"*

*This is almost too much for her. The bride is having such a difficult time paying attention because her heart is overflowing walking so close to Him. She whispers, "Dear Husband, my heart is about to burst. Forgive me for not speaking." It was a greater fullness of her spirit than she had ever experienced. **Arm in arm they continued walking.** Pausing, the Beloved breathes in the magnificent fragrance, then, with one sweep of His hand over the garden, He says, "Your garden, look at it My love..."*

God's Ring

I have a ring I am very fond of that I wear everyday and it just happens to be white gold. I lost my ring one day and I looked through the washer twice and could not find it. I looked everywhere for this ring that day. The next morning to my relief, I opened the dryer door and saw my ring sitting on the rim. This was so strange. Then, that same afternoon this was the section I came to in reading my *"Devotional Commentary on the Song of Solomon"* and what I was reading was all about a gold ring—something that coincidently I had been focusing on for the entire day when my own ring was missing. Here is the copy from the book:

Song of Solomon 5:14: *His hands are as **gold rings** set with the beryl: his belly is as bright ivory overlaid with sapphires.*

"Rings" –no beginning or ending! Whatever the Beloved, eternal God touches it must respond to Him. Whatever He accomplishes with His hands it is an infinite, eternal work! Thank You dear Lord, since we

are in Your hand, then we are encircled by Your "gold rings." O the security, the comfort, the assurance, the peaceful shelter in being surrounded by His hands; to be totally encompassed by God Himself! People wear rings to display their symbolic value, beauty or cherished meaning. Is that not what the Beloved will be doing with His bride in Revelations 21:1-11? Glory to God! How befitting that we should be part of His ring ("beryl").

Holy Seal

One time in the car ride home from school with my son Ethan, I discovered he had found an old wax seal that I had not seen for a long time. It said S.W.A.K. (sealed with a kiss) on it and my son wanted to know what S.W.A.K. meant and what was its use? Then he asked me if people still used these and I said, "Well occasionally." Then I launched into this whole description of how kings used them for sealing official documents and they used their own unique seal mark so people would know it was officially from them only. After this discussion that day, you can see what I ran into the very next day, of all things, in the *"Devotional Commentary on the Song of Solomon"* reading (again, I had completely no foreknowledge that I would be reading anything about this at all):

Song of Solomon 8:6: *Set me as a seal upon thine heart, as a seal upon thine arm:* for love is strong as death; jealousy is cruel as the grave: the coals thereof are coals of fire, which hath a most vehement flame.

*The Lord Jesus, your heavenly Bridegroom speaks to you... "Set me as a **seal** upon thine heart, as a seal upon thine arm: for love is strong as death; jealousy is cruel (severe, unyielding) as the grave: the coals (Hebrews "flames") thereof are coals (flames) of fire, which hath a most vehement flame (of the Lord). The word "seal" is the same Hebrew word for "signet" or "signet ring." The king (or his representative) would affix the royal seal to a document representing His authority, will, ownership, protection or direction. It was to be permanent! **Esther 8:8** is a wonderful example of this: "Write ye...in the king's name, and seal it with the king's ring: for the writing which is written in the king's name, and sealed with the king's ring, may no man reverse."*

*The seal from King Jesus today is the Holy Spirit (**2 Corinthians 1:22; Ephesians 1:13; 4:30**)! The Holy Spirit is the seal placed within us and assures us that what God promises in His word He will perform! That "sealing of the Holy Spirit" took place the moment she received her Beloved as her personal Lord and Savior. In this verse, He is asking her to set Him as a seal upon her heart and arm. She looked very puzzled at this request from Him.*

He explains, "My darling bride your heart must have My seal upon it for that is where you make your decisions. Then it must be put on your arm that carries them out. With each decision you must place My seal upon it, then nothing will ever come between us as we walk together up out of this wilderness. It will demonstrate more than anything else that you love Me with all of your heart."

So amazingly, I spoke to my son about a king's signet ring and the importance of the seal—only to read all about the seal of the Holy Spirit that Christ places on His beloved the next day. Here are some more verses about kings' seals found in the Bible:

Daniel 6:17: *And a stone was brought, and laid upon the mouth of the den; and the king sealed it with his own signet, and with the signet of his lords; that the purpose might not be changed concerning Daniel.*

Genesis 41:42: *And Pharaoh took off his ring from his hand, and put it upon Joseph's hand, and arrayed him in vestures of fine linen, and put a gold chain about his neck;*

Esther 3:10: *And the king took his ring from his hand, and gave it unto Haman the son of Hammedatha the Agagite, the Jews' enemy.*

Esther 8:2: *And the king took off his ring, which he had taken from Haman, and gave it unto Mordecai. And Esther set Mordecai over the house of Haman.*

Esther 8:8: *Write ye also for the Jews, as it liketh you, in the king's name, and seal it with the king's ring: for the writing which is written in the king's name, and sealed with the king's ring, may no man reverse.*

Esther 8:10: *And he wrote in the king Ahasuerus' name, and sealed it with the king's ring, and sent letters by posts on horseback, and riders on mules, camels, and young dromedaries:*

Haggai 2:23: *In that day, saith the LORD of hosts, will I take thee, O Zerubbabel, my servant, the son of Shealtiel, saith the LORD, and will make thee as a signet: for I have chosen thee, saith the LORD of hosts.*

Ephesians 1:13: *In whom ye also trusted, after that ye heard the word of truth, the gospel of your salvation: in whom also after that ye believed, ye were sealed with that holy Spirit of promise,*

Ephesians 4:30: *And grieve not the holy Spirit of God, whereby ye are sealed unto the day of redemption.*

2 Corinthians 1:21-22: *Now he which stablisheth us with you in Christ, and hath anointed us, is God; Who hath also sealed us, and given the earnest of the Spirit in our hearts.*

No One Can Snatch Us!

I was home praying and during my prayer, I cited aloud the verse from the Bible to God about how *"No one can snatch us out of His hand"* (quoted from **John 10:28**).

Well a little bit later, I went downstairs for lunch. I began to read the *"Devotional Commentary on the Song of Solomon"* and amazingly this is one of the first verses, in the study, I turned to next:

Her Beloved's eyes sparkled with delight. Intently gazing at His hands He slowly opened the palms exposing the scars and said, "My faithful bride these are the seal for you, the scars of My crucifixion. They are the guarantee that I will never leave you nor forsake you. They are the assurance that My love for you is eternal. ***They are My pledge that your sins will never rise again to condemn you and the safety that no one can snatch you out of them (John 10:28)!*** *My Spirit's indescribable power will be released in you! Then you will know My love which surpasses knowledge (**Ephesians 3:19**). You will be filled with all the fullness of God (**Ephesians 3:19**) and be transformed from glory to glory in Me" (**2 Corinthians 3:18**).*

I found this **Song of Solomon** study to be amazing just like so many of Jesus' parables and the classic tale *"Pilgrim's Progress,"* written as a parable by John Bunyan. So much is revealed in this Holy of Holies book of the Bible. It is a love letter written to the Bride (the true Church of Christ and/or individual Christian) from her Bridegroom (Jesus). The revelations in this book to the author were miraculous as well as my experiences while reading it. I had experienced miraculous things apart from this book in my walk to go deeper with Christ—but this was an extraordinary experience and all those who follow hard after Christ will benefit so much from taking this walk…

There was yet another time this wonderful verse came to my attention. As I was home watching a Christian movie on TV, I was also checking my email on my laptop. The woman in the TV movie was reciting the verse **John 10:27-28.** I was checking my email *at the same time* and I had received my email devotion. It popped up with the same identical verses the woman on TV was quoting exactly **John 10:27-28!** These two events happened within seconds of the other. It was surreal.

John 10:27-28: *My sheep hear my voice, and I know them, and they follow me: And I give unto them eternal life; and they shall never perish, neither shall any man pluck them out of my hand.*

Struggling with Sin

Amazingly, this happens to me frequently—sometimes even daily that I will be reading two completely different books with two completely different subjects—and then something like this happens…

I was reading the *"Devotional Commentary on the Song of Solomon"* and the other book was written by author John Piper titled *"The Pleasures of God—Meditations on God's Delight in Being God."*

Now here is the fascinating thing, I was reading two different books and yet within the same day, the topics of both sections I was in tell the same exact message, covering the same subject and even sometimes quoting the same verses. Really, what are the chances of this? Each chapter, in each book is uniquely different as each book is and yet, I read the same message in each book simultaneously. Incredible! The message from each book was regarding our ever-present struggle with sin as seen in **Romans 7:14-20:**

Paul writes in **Romans 7:14-20:** *For we know that the law is spiritual: but I am carnal, sold under sin. For that which I do I allow not: for what I would, that do I not; but what I hate, that do I. If then I do that which I would not, I consent unto the law that it is good. Now then it is no more I that do it, but sin that dwelleth in me. For I know that in me (that is, in my flesh,) dwelleth no good thing: for to will is present with me; but how to perform that which is good I find not. For the good that I would I do not: but the evil which I would not, that I do. Now if I do that I would not, it is no more I that do it, but sin that dwelleth in me.*

I liken this understanding about our sin to a cat attached to a tree, hanging only by its claws (in which we are like the cat hanging onto our ways of doing things with our claws). The cat's owner (God) walks up and is willingly available to allow the cat (us) to jump safely into His arms (away from our struggle with sinning). The cat surveys the situation while slipping and wonders whether or not to trust the owner standing by or continue to hang on with the claws it depends on so heavily (striving against sin apart from God's help). For a moment, the cat remembers the trustworthiness of the owner providing food and shelter. It releases its grip and belief in its own ability to save itself and jumps by faith into the arms of its owner—the one who has loved it all along. The cat can rest in the owner's arms of safety.

Both point out that God never meant for us to strive, but to rush into His arms, trust Him for our salvation and faith to be obedient in the way He requires us to live. Even though we are involved—it is never about us—we cannot do it—we cannot redeem ourselves and we cannot *go and sin no more* apart from Christ either.

Chapter Twenty—Commitment to Fullness

Commitment to Fullness

Although I was a committed Christian, I put a lot of stock in my career as the center of my life. I know that God wanted me to make Him the primary focus of my life. I was very discouraged with the company that I had been working for and I could never understand why I seemed to be the only one who was not paid for the work I did.

I used to pray to God about this situation all the time. Then next, I worked on the "Harvest Show" project along with Retha McPherson and her business partner Manie du Toit, who came to town and he hardly knew me because we had just met. Manie, a former professional rugby player, came from South Africa with Retha McPherson who I was hosting while she was scheduled to be on the "Harvest Show" in South Bend, Indiana to promote her miraculous book *"Message from God."*

When I met Manie for the first time, he walked up to me and said that God had some money to give me. I told him that I could not accept it and that I was not expecting to receive any pay for helping them with this project. He insisted and once again, I told him that I was not seeking monetary gain for helping them. Then Manie said to me, "No you don't understand." "God has instructed me to give you this money," and he handed me a check for the exact amount that I had always been praying to God to be paid by my current employer. I was dumbstruck and completely overwhelmed. Manie knew nothing about this at all because we had just met. Manie, a man I barely knew, instructed me that God wanted me to work for God now.

God also had asked Manie to give up his career to work for God. Manie now has a marvelous ministry called Living Balls spreading the gospel of Christ through the message of Jesus on soccer and other sport balls to children in African villages and in other countries. For details about Manie's ministry, visit www.livingballs.com.

Not long after this wonderful event, I ran across a kind of declaration that I had signed back in the previous year and it was a commitment I made to turn my life over to God. *Now in this paper it said that God would put me under a strict watch and He would bring my finances to a point where I would see that it was God supplying me with my needs and no one else.* When I found this document I had signed (which I had gotten through my church), I wept like a baby. I realized that this was God at work in my life, pulling me away from my self-dependency on my career and pursuit of the world for my security, which was driving me apart from God. I realized that God was trying to tell me something because it was bizarre the way I ran across this paper at the same time I had received the check from Manie for the exact amount I was not able to obtain from my employer.

Now I wish I could say that I walked away from my career and focused on God at this point. But, that did not happen. I stayed on with my employer and I did not take Manie's or God's advice. My job at the time was promoting parties for children. One Sunday evening, I was home and reading John Bunyan's classic book, *"Pilgrim's Progress."* Essentially Bunyan's book is a parable focusing on the life of a Christian and the many perilous hazards he faces. As I was reading, I received an interesting call...

A reporter called from another city inquiring about the children's parties I promoted and he asked if the company I worked for offered magic parties for kids because he loved magic. **I explained that the closest thing we offered were wizard parties** (now do not forget this part). Then we completed our call and the reporter hung up. In a hurry, I turned back to reading the *"Pilgrim's Progress"* book where I had left off.

Right after hanging up from the call with the reporter, I turned the page in the book and *at the top of the next page*, the copy read how GOD HATED WIZARDS. I was totally checked in my spirit and realized that God had been trying to get me to leave this job and that I needed to turn to God and work for Him. And, that is what I did and this time I did so right away. I knew I did not want any affiliation with promoting the affection for the occult to children.

Deuteronomy 18:10-13: says: *There shall not be found among you any one that maketh his son or his daughter to pass through the fire, or that useth divination, or an observer of times, or an enchanter, or a witch. Or a charmer, or a consulter with familiar spirits,* ***or a wizard,*** *or a necromancer.* ***For all that do these things are an abomination unto the LORD****: and because of these abominations the LORD thy God doth drive them out from before thee. Thou shalt be perfect with the LORD thy God.*

Matthew 18:6: *But whoso shall offend one of these little ones which believe in me, it were better for him that a millstone were hanged about his neck, and that he were drowned in the depth of the sea.*

Here is a copy of the amazing *Commitment to Fullness in Christ* document that I had signed the year before:

Commitment to Fullness in Christ*

If God has called you to be truly like Jesus, he will draw you into a life of crucifixion and humility and put on you demands of obedience that sometimes will not allow you to follow other Christians. In many ways, he will seem to let other good people do things He will not let you do.

Other Christians and even ministers, who seem very religious and useful, may push themselves, pull strings and work schemes to carry out their plans, but you cannot do these things, and if you attempt them, you will meet with such failure and rebuke from the Lord as to make you sorry you did.

Others can brag about themselves, about their work, about their successes, about their writings, but the Holy Spirit will not allow you to do such things: and if you begin bragging, He will lead you into some deep mortification that will make you despise yourself and all your good works.

Others will be allowed to succeed in making great sums of money, or having a legacy left to them, or in having luxuries, but God may only supply you daily, because He wants you to have something better than gold—a helpless dependence on Him—that He may have the privilege of providing your needs daily out of the unseen treasury.

The Lord may let others be honored and keep you hidden away in obscurity, because He wants to produce some choice, fragrant fruit for His coming glory, which can only be produced in the shade.

God will let others be great, but keep you small. He will let others do a work for Him, and get the credit for it, but He will make you work and toil without knowing how much you are doing. And then to make your work more precious, He will let others get the credit for the work which you have done, and this will make your reward ten times greater when Jesus comes.

The Holy Spirit will put a strict watch on you, with jealous love, and rebuke you for little words and feelings for wasted time, which other Christians never seem distressed over.

With this in mind, I make up my mind that God is an infinite Sovereign who has a right to do as He pleases with His own, and needs not explain to me a thousand things, which may puzzle my reason in His dealing with me.

God, take me at my word, I absolutely yield myself to be Your slave, to be wrapped up in a jealous love, to let other people say and do many things I cannot do, but I only want to do your will.

I settle it that I am to deal directly with the Holy and that He is to have the privilege of tying my tongue or chaining my hand or closing my eyes in ways that others are not disciplined.

Now, possess me so with fullness in Christ, that I am in my secret heart, pleased and delighted over this peculiar, personal, private, jealous guardianship and management of the Holy Spirit over my life, that I would truly live in the vestibule of Heaven.

May what I make as a covenant on earth between God, and me be ratified in Heaven.

Signed _____ Date _____

Adapted from an unknown source

So the challenge is before you as it was for me. Are you willing to hand over your life and surrender to Christ? You do not have to sign this form to be committed to Christ—but you do need to repent to Jesus of your sins and submit your life to Him willingly. It is not the easiest choice—but it is the best choice you will ever make. Remember, the pay off on this decision will be eternal.

Rising Out of the Ashes

The past few years have been challenging for me and I had to make some difficult major personal decisions and changes. On one Sunday morning upon first waking, I heard the Lord say to me, ***"Rising out of the ashes."*** I thought I had better look that phrase up, but then I had a very busy Sunday schedule at church and numerous activities so I completely forgot what I had heard.

Then late, that same evening, I was online checking my email and I decided to look up some information about God that I wanted to find. I stumbled onto a website with a list of articles and interestingly one had the heading, *"Rising Out of the Ashes."* Seeing the article heading triggered my memory from the words I had heard the Lord say that very morning: ***"Rising out of the ashes."*** I decided to read that particular article of the same heading and it was simply saying that God can take us and use us even when we experience failure and this I believe is what God was trying to tell me. This was truly amazing. I know God wanted me to get this message and it really spoke to my situation at the time. This is the summary of that article: *Sometimes everything in your life is destroyed and all you have left is ashes. Fortunately, as a Christian, God has a way of making something beautiful out of your ashes.*

I can assure you that up to this point in my life, I had become completely enamored with pursing success through money and position. God had compassion on me and buried me in the ashes of my own self-made idolatry. After losing my identity tied to my focus on work, God stepped in and brought me down low so that I could see what I had become and allowed me to die to myself and to seek answers for my life that can only be found through Him.

Isaiah 61:1-4: *The Spirit of the Lord GOD is upon me; because the LORD hath anointed me to preach good tidings unto the meek; he hath sent me to bind up the brokenhearted, to proclaim liberty to the captives, and the opening of the prison to them that are bound; To proclaim the acceptable year of the LORD, and the day of vengeance of our God; to comfort all that mourn; To appoint unto them that mourn in Zion, to give unto them beauty for ashes, the oil of joy for mourning, the garment of praise for the spirit of heaviness; that they might be called trees of righteousness, the planting of the LORD, that he might be glorified.*

"Read Deuteronomy"

One morning early, before I had any of my own thoughts formed in my head, I woke and immediately I heard the Holy Spirit say to me the audible words, ***"Read Deuteronomy."*** I was amazed because the thought of reading specifically Deuteronomy could not have been further from my mind—especially at that early hour first thing in the morning and any day prior. So, I contemplated briefly on what I heard and I rolled over and fell asleep for at least another hour. Then the next time I awoke an hour later that same morning, I heard the Holy Spirit speak to me immediately, distinctly, and simply, ***"Read Deuteronomy."*** Again, I was amazed to hear so clearly these words imploring me to read Deuteronomy the second time.

The next morning rolled around and as I awoke, immediately I heard for the third, and final time, the Holy Spirit's voice clearly say, **"Read Deuteronomy."** Moreover, I was surprised and amazed regarding the third request for me to read Deuteronomy. As you can imagine I was compelled to read Deuteronomy willingly taking the guidance of the Holy Spirit, my Spiritual Counselor.

This was shocking to me because I had not even been contemplating reading Deuteronomy at all. And looking back on this unique request of God, I realized that overall the Book of Deuteronomy was written by Moses as sermons to the Israelites prior to their entering the Promised Land and how they were challenged by new temptations and trials. In Deuteronomy, Moses goes over the Ten Commandments with his people and discusses the upsides of following God and the downsides of turning from Him. Deuteronomy is very much a book that outlines the basics of God's expectations of His children. Therefore, I highly recommend all Christians to "read Deuteronomy." I was being instructed to further understand the laws, that guided the Israelites so long ago, and that still stand for this generation so many years later.

Because we now have the mercy and grace of God restored by the shedding of Christ's blood on the cross, we are now compelled to follow the law given by God because of our *love* for Him. We cannot live by God's law apart from frequent repentance to God for our daily sin and for the help from the Holy Spirit who comes to reside in us *after we first surrender ourselves fully to Christ.* God gives His laws to us to follow, Christ then redeems us through His blood for our failure to follow the laws in our own strength. And the Holy Spirit comes into us and guides us in getting to know and love God to the point where through His strength alone we long to follow His laws.

2 Timothy 1:13-14: *Hold fast the form of sound words, which thou hast heard of me, in faith and love which is in Christ Jesus. That good thing which was committed unto thee keep by the Holy Ghost which dwelleth in us.*

White Stone

At the point in time I was beginning to think that I might actually write a book, I was in my car on the way to my Sunday morning church service, and a most extraordinary thought came to my mind. I thought about the verse **Revelations 2:17**, which reads:

*He that hath an ear, let him hear what the Spirit saith unto the churches; To him that overcometh will I give to eat of the hidden manna, **and will give him a white stone, and in the stone a new name written, which no man knoweth saving he that receiveth it.***

I remember it like it was yesterday… I was pulling out of my driveway, and I thought about this verse. How beautiful it is that God gives us a white stone with a name written on it only known between God and the recipient. I thought this verse really shows the wonderfully, romantic side of God. I felt that somehow, I definitely wanted to include this particular verse in my book.

Revelations 2:17 was the verse on my mind when church started that same morning. To my utter amazement, at my morning church service the congregational reading verse was **Revelations 2:12-17** *and our Pastor's sermon was all about **Revelations 2:12-17**!* Okay to say I was floored was an understatement. I still think this is something quite remarkable! I had no advance knowledge that our Pastor would deliver his service on **Revelations 2:17**.

Jesus, King of Kings

One time, I was in my car talking away to Jesus and I was traveling on a road I had been down many, many times everyday. My conversation turned to how I had trouble comprehending that Jesus was not only my best friend but also a King! While driving through an intersection I had been traveling through, too many times to count, the most amazing thing happened. As I made my statement to Christ how He was not just my friend but also a King, I immediately noticed that someone had placed a large, handwritten sign with the word "KING" in all caps to sell a king mattress. This sign had never been there before and had just been placed on the corner since the last time I had driven through the intersection. However, it was incredible the way I commented on Christ being a King and *at that very moment,* I saw a sign with "KING" on it (when previously that sign had never been there before). This really threw me for a loop. Had I said the word King a little sooner, or later, I would not have seen the sign at the same time I said the word KING—the timing was just incredible.

Revelation 19:16: *And he hath on his vesture and on his thigh a name written, KING OF KINGS, AND LORD OF LORDS.*

"Help Me with My Unbelief!"

In April of 2008, I decided to pray to the Lord for serious help over a specific situation that was very stressful to me. During my prayer, I mentioned a phrase I remembered from a story in the Bible about a father who approached Christ with a request to heal his son from demon possession. Jesus stated that everything is possible for him who believes. In the story, the father exclaimed, "I do believe; help me overcome my unbelief!" I think all followers at some point in their walk with Christ have really wanted to believe in the abilities of Christ, yet had doubts the same way this man did. That morning, I shared that same doubt while praying and I pleaded with the Lord THREE times in these words:

"I do believe; help me with my unbelief!"

I remember doing this as if it were yesterday.

After this precious time praying to God, I finished feeling better and I tripped on downstairs to my laptop to check the day's email messages. I was *stunned,* when I opened my daily email devotion that arrived and it was all about verses **Mark 9:22-24**. This devotion was all about the exact phrase I had just uttered in my prayer THREE times (*I do believe; help me with my unbelief!*) *right before* I checked my email.

Now some might conclude that this was an incredible coincidence. However, what exactly are the chances that this particular verse could pop up in my random devotional email that morning after citing the same verse in my prayer three times? Given that the average Bible has 31,173 verses, it makes it startling that such an occurrence could take place. Here is that story in the Bible that I referred to in my prayer and the same one that showed up in my email that morning:

Mark 9:17-26: *And one of the multitude answered and said, Master, I have brought unto thee my son, which hath a dumb spirit; And wheresoever he taketh him, he teareth him: and he foameth, and gnasheth with his teeth, and pineth away: and I spake to thy disciples that they should cast him out; and they could not. He answereth him, and saith, O faithless generation, how long shall I be with you? how long shall I suffer you? Bring him unto me. And they brought him unto him: and when he saw him, straightway the spirit tare him; and he fell on the ground, and wallowed foaming. And he asked his father, How long is it ago since this came unto him? And he said, Of a child. And ofttimes it hath cast him into the fire, and into the waters, to destroy him: but if thou canst do anything, have compassion on us, and help us. Jesus said unto him, If thou canst believe, all things are possible to him that believeth. And straightway the father of the child cried out, and said with tears,*

Lord, I believe; help thou mine unbelief.

When Jesus saw that the people came running together, he rebuked the foul spirit, saying unto him, Thou dumb and deaf spirit, I charge thee, come out of him, and enter no more into him. And the spirit cried, and rent him sore, and came out of him: and he was as one dead; insomuch that many said, He is dead.

Taking Communion

Back in July of 2008, my son and I were at the local Christian bookstore looking around. I was in one part of the store and Ethan another part. He told me after we were there just a few minutes that during the time we were in the store the Lord spoke to him and told him to take communion every day. We are in a store, and Ethan is usually concerned about the toys or things he can find—the last thing he would be thinking about is whether one should take communion everyday or not. At the time I thought, okay this is odd and interesting.

I was amazed about what Ethan had told me he had heard, because later in August, when I had heard the minister Perry Stone on TV talking about the revival he felt was coming for God to impress on His people the custom of the first Christians of taking communion in their homes every day. And, with repentance and communion there was healing of health, spirit, and emotions, and greater intimacy with God. So this is interesting that God would have told this to Ethan.

Funny because after seeing the Perry Stone program about taking communion everyday, on the next morning, our Sunday service we took communion and the sermon was about this verse:

1 Corinthians 11:24-25: *And when he had given thanks, he brake it, and said, Take, eat: this is my body, which is broken for you: this do in remembrance of me. After the same manner also he took the cup, when he had supped, saying, this cup is the new testament in my blood: this do ye, as often as ye drink it, in remembrance of me.*

Now that I take communion every day that I am able, I focus on a theme to honor Christ's sacrifice. Here are some of the themes I have contemplated on during each communion: Christ's courage; Christ's perseverance; Christ's incredible love; Christ's passion; Christ's resolve to go through with the crucifixion; Christ's sacrifice; and Christ's completeness as the perfect sacrifice. When you daily repent to God for your sins and take Holy Communion, you too can remember all the things Christ's gift through death has meant to you.

Praise the Lord

While checking my email for the day, I received my Daily Devotional email featuring the **103rd Psalms** with **verses 1-12**. At the time I thought to myself how much this particular Psalms was speaking to me that day in some things going on in my life. I really liked this verse, so instead of just deleting it, I chose to save it so I could reread it again later.

A little while that same day, I decided to read from a book I had been reading titled *"One Holy Passion"* by R. C. Sproul and (with no prior knowledge of what I was about to read), I read a couple pages and then turned the page to find the **103rd Psalms verses 1-12** featured in the book. I thought to myself, "Wait a minute…why is that sounding so familiar?" I realized that I had just read these exact verses in my Daily Devotional email earlier that morning. What makes this even more amazing is that **Psalms 103** has *22 verses altogether*, but oddly in both of these two instances, *only verses 1-12 are mentioned and not all 22 verses.*

How could it be that I would receive a devotional email featuring a particular group of verses only to turn around and read from a book focusing *on the content of the exact same 12 verses from the Bible*—of all the many verses in the Bible, on that same day? Here are the verses I read in both amazing instances that morning:

Psalms 103: 1-12: *Bless the LORD, O my soul: and all that is within me, bless his holy name. Bless the LORD, O my soul, and forget not all his benefits: Who forgiveth all thine iniquities; who healeth all thy diseases; Who redeemeth thy life from destruction; who crowneth thee with lovingkindness and tender mercies; Who satisfieth thy mouth with good things; so that thy youth is renewed like the eagle's. The LORD executeth righteousness and judgment for all that are oppressed. He made known his ways unto Moses, his acts unto the children of Israel. The LORD is merciful and gracious, slow to anger, and plenteous in mercy. He will not always chide: neither will he keep his anger forever. He hath not dealt with us after our sins; nor rewarded us according to our iniquities. For as the heaven is high above the earth, so great is his mercy toward them that fear him. As far as the east is from the west, so far hath he removed our transgressions from us.*

Mustard Seed

Now early in the day, I was praying to the Lord about a matter of my weak faith. Moreover, I suggested at least *three* times to the Lord how I knew that if I just had a mustard seed size-faith that the Lord would take care of the rest. I must have referred to the mustard seed at least *three* times during my prayer time.

I keep several pieces of jewelry in some tiny toy teacups on my bathroom sink in a bunch. In that teacup was an old bracelet my mother owned and it had a single charm on it: a locket, which you can see clearly, a single mustard seed. Now that same night, right before I was getting ready for bed I went to the bathroom and to my shock, I found my mustard seed bracelet out of the teacup and laying on my bathroom counter all by itself. I nearly swallowed my own tongue when I saw the bracelet sitting by the sink.

I quizzed my family about the bracelet and neither one knew anything about it. I asked them again if they were sure and they said they had not set it out on the counter. I cannot say, how it was sitting out by itself on my bathroom counter but only that I found it and I had not set it out myself. I can only say that it was amazing to find a mustard seed bracelet after pleading with God numerous times earlier that day that I knew that all I needed was a mustard seed size-faith and that God can do the rest. Here is that verse from the Bible:

Matthew 17:20: *And Jesus said unto them, Because of your unbelief: for verily I say unto you, If ye have faith as a grain of mustard seed, ye shall say unto this mountain, Remove hence to yonder place; and it shall remove; and nothing shall be impossible unto you.*

God's Plans

As always, God amazes me...you know I was talking away to Him in the car one morning and I said something specifically to Him about plans for my life. I said, "You know, I hope you have included me in your plans and if not, I hope you can rearrange your plans to include me!" Okay I was sort of messing around—but this is amazing, *within an hour* of this conversation I was reading a book and this verse came up:

Jeremiah 29:11: *For I know the thoughts that I think toward you, saith the LORD, thoughts of peace, and not of evil, to give you an expected end.*

Chapter Twenty-one—Beautiful Words

Beautiful Words

To understand a recent experience I had, you must know a little about the background first. Previously in this book, I told of the research paper about Heaven I did originally for myself that later ended up being sent to many people. One woman I know wanted a copy of my research paper and she lives as far as Belgium. To protect her identity I am going to refer to her as "Mrs. Anonymous." Now "Mrs. Anonymous" and I developed a friendship over the year after I had shared my data with her. She is a very Holy Spirit-filled woman who also is an enthusiastic follower of Christ. She had revealed to me that she had a unique gift of hearing from the Lord for encouraging others. Over the past year I communicated with "Mrs. Anonymous," she shared her highs and lows of communicating her faith with the lost people who lived around her and her enthusiasm over witnessing to others about Jesus.

I had realized that the Lord was showing me (as He is many others) that He is coming soon and that we are living in the end times. Recently, I had shared this information with a friend who is in ministry work. This individual, I later believed did not seem to be too concerned that we are in the end times and I found this to be very discouraging.

I wrote an email to some close friends about my deep sadness that my friend who I had spoken to about the Lord's soon return was seemingly not concerned about it.

In my email to my friends, I had written a list of things that I believed will go wrong in the world if the Lord does not return soon. This includes the rapid growth of evil worldwide among other things. Now I emailed my frustrations about this also to my friend in Belgium, "Mrs. Anonymous." I do not know what I expected her response to be—but I could not have been prepared for the response I received from her.

"Mrs. Anonymous" wrote me back and she said that the Lord was speaking to her with a word for me to address my frustration. Because her first language is Dutch and not American English, Christ spoke to her in Dutch and as He spoke a message to her for me, she translated it into American English. For the reason of authenticity, I am going to leave the letter as I received it in its actual uncorrected translated form:

Dear Susan,

I believe the Lord wants to encourage you. He is talking to me right now to write this down for you:

*"My precious daughter, I see your grief. I see your sorrows. I know them all, from the inside and from the outside. But I tell you My dear child, don't be discouraged. I shall take care of you and for your son and for your husband and for your entire family. I tell you, don't be worried! I am the Lord who created you. I Am the I Am. Nothing happens out of My perfect will. Listen carefully: DON'T LOOK AT THE CIRCUMSTANCES! Did you hear Me? DON'T LOOK AT THE CIRCUMSTANCES! Keep your eyes fixed on Me. I am the Lord who takes care of you. I am the Lord who loves you. **I am your Finisher.** My dear child, keep your eyes fixed on Me. The devil does everything to discourage you. I have seen the work you have done for Me. Everything is noted in My book. I shall not condemn you My precious daughter. Cause that's what you are, My precious daughter. Believe My daughter that these are My words for you. I tell you again, keep your eyes fixed on ME! Not on the circumstances. I love you My child and I will take care of you till the day I come back. Believe that I am coming soon. Many will be surprised. But I know you won't be surprised, because your heart desires to see Me. Continue to pray My lovely child and continue to do what you are doing. I look only to the heart and I see that your heart is good. Don't give up My child! I tell*

you, I AM COMING SOON! Sooner than many people think. Let them go up in their theories. One day they will be very surprised and they will miss the greatest feast ever: The wedding of the Lamb. Do whatever you are doing My daughter, your wages are waiting for you in Heaven. Look at Me, keep your eyes fixed on Me!"

If you want to, please tell me how you received this.
(Signed "Mrs. Anonymous"—name changed to protect my friend's identity)

I had written to my friend in Belgium that when in her letter to me from the Lord that He had said *"I am your Finisher"* this had significant meaning to me because when I talk to Him, I frequently quote the verse to HIM that He is the "Author and Finisher of my faith"

I used to have serious doubts about my salvation and when I ran across **Hebrews 12:2,** I was so excited that Jesus is the Author and "Finisher" of our faith. Many, many times **I would often talk to Him reminding Him that He is "The Finisher!" and calling Him that all the time.** *I had never told anyone else this. It was exclusively between me and Christ.* Here is Hebrews 12:2:

*Looking unto Jesus the **author and finisher of our faith**; who for the joy that was set before him endured the cross, despising the shame, and is set down at the right hand of the throne of God.*

My friend, "Mrs. Anonymous" from Belgium wrote me back about the reference to the "Finisher":

Susan,

Let me give you a little more information about my mail to you yesterday. When I was reading your mail where you said you were so discouraged by something your friend said, the Lord immediately spoke to me and told me that He would answer you through me. I finished reading your mail. This is how it worked: I just was sitting at my computer and the Lord spoke to me in Dutch, sentence by sentence and I just wrote it down in English for you. I could translate immediately. I also felt I could not wait too long to send you the mail, that is why I first sent you a short one to let you know the Lord had a word for you. I asked the Lord not to use too many difficult words, so I could translate easily for you and send you the mail quickly.

To answer your questions:
Yes, the Lord told me these are His words for you! Believe me, it is most amazing for me too.

Yes, the Lord gives me messages for others too. The first time was a few years ago. He gave me I think seven letters for someone who had a hard time and the Lord told her she would be raptured alive, after giving her advice for emotional healing. What she does with this advice is up to her, I only spoke the words of the Lord. But these letters were very encouraging and full of His love.

After that, the Lord used me to help some more people (but not that much) to answer by mail to encourage them or sometimes He even gives me a prayer for them or even advice. One time, one person felt that the depression was gone right after reading a prayer the Lord gave me. Until now, everyone answers that they feel the presence and power of the Holy Spirit through the words of the Lord and they feel like a burden is taken off.

The bottom line is that He said He would use this gift (hearing His Voice) for others as a prophetic voice. I am very honored He wants to use me for this. I thank the wonderful precious Holy Spirit who speaks to me the words of Jesus. I can understand you when you say that this does not sound like my voice, but the Lord's. I always want to stay humble in my speaking to people.

When he told me the part that He is *"your Finisher,"* I doubted for a second, because I do not use this word a lot. *However, He told me not to doubt and just write it down for you.* So I see this as a nice confirmation, because it means something to you!

I capped the section "DON'T LOOK AT THE CIRCUMSTANCES" because the Lord told me to do it this way, to cap them! Amazing isn't it? I do nothing out of myself when I write to someone; everything I do is from the Lord. Even when He pauses for a little moment or speaks slower, I use a, to make sure the accent is in the letter. Sometimes I can feel His mood, when He is enthusiastic, oh the Lord can be very enthusiastic and then I mention it afterwards, so the person knows.

Believe it Susan, the Lord is talking to you this way, why wouldn't He? You are the most precious thing on the earth for Him (my words!), but this is the truth. Yes, the Lord hears everything you say to Him, He is always there with you and your prayers are heard in Heaven. Just believe this. The Lord speaks to everybody, but in different ways.

Well anyway, I can say I hear the voice of the Lord all the time. I would not say this in the beginning, but the Lord gave me permission a while ago to do it. So now, I do it, but I try to stay humble and I do not tell people this just like that, because I know they would not believe me. I just know He has His purpose for this and one of them is to speak about His coming, which has begun in my church. Another one is that people may enjoy this wonderful gift He gave me by encouraging them or helping them. The Lord although does not always answer every question. He just says what they need to hear at that moment. Also in my life, He does not give me too many details at once, because it is important I keep my peace and stay relaxed (two conditions to hear His voice), because He knows I get enthusiastic very quickly!

Please enjoy with these words, I enjoy with you big time!

I then wrote back my friend in Belgium this message:
In addition, when I gave this message to my son—he wept because he had just prayed to God a couple days before about needing assurance that he would go to Heaven. This was a wonderful answer to his prayer. I did not know he had prayed for this assurance from the Lord.

I told you why this letter from the Lord was so extraordinary, because He used the words *"I am your Finisher."* This amazed me because I have many times quoted the verse that the Lord is the *Author* and *Finisher* of my faith. I talk to Him all the time that He is the *Finisher* of my faith. Well He used that line *"I am your Finisher"*—I love it—I love it.

Therefore, I was reading over this letter the next night because it is so precious to me of course—and when I came to that word *"Finisher"*—the person speaking in the movie, that was on TV in the room at the time said the word, *"FINISHED"* exactly when I read the word *"FINISHER."* What a phenomenal confirmation!

After receiving this letter, a couple of my friends insisted that I include this wonderful message in my book and I was reluctant to consider doing it without the express permission from the woman who received the message for me from the Lord. Therefore, I wrote her a note and I asked her to pray about my request. I assured her that if this were not in God's will, then I would abandon the idea and be happy to keep the letter to myself. She wrote back and agreed to pray about it. Surprisingly, I received a response the next day.

"Mrs. Anonymous" wrote this:
I have prayed for your question and I believe this is what the Lord tells me:

"My precious child, do not be worried about how or what you will be making your book. Everything you have on your heart is good. I shall work everything out and I will give My blessing to everything. My Spirit will lead you. Ask for His leading and He will do it. Your heart is good my daughter. Don't hold yourself to put all My testimonies in your book. Finish it and do it fast. I am coming very, very soon. I want you to know that I shall protect your son; his little heart is very pleasing for Me. You will be raptured together. Hold yourself ready, because behold, I am coming very, very soon!"

Susan, I asked the Lord if it is okay to put the letter He gave to you in your book and He said it is okay. Like He mentioned above (how wonderful again), you can do whatever you have on your heart with your book. He gives you His freedom in this and He will bless it. *Do it fast and keep yourself ready for the rapture.* This is what He tells me again right now.

Susan, I feel that the Lord has a lot of love for your son, please tell him that! It will encourage him. Sometimes when I pray or when the Lord speaks to me for people as He just did now for you, He allows me to feel His heart and I feel He loves the heart of that little boy of yours! Thank You Jesus.

Well, you have the Lord's approval to put the letter He gave you in your book, and it is indeed not necessary to put my name under it, because it is the Lord's letter, so put His name under it if you want. All praise and honour goes to Him!

This is what the Lord says: *"My precious daughter, this letter was meant for you personally to encourage and confirm you, but if you use it in your book, it shall bless also other people."*

Here you go, the Lord is willing to answer right away. This is so amazing.

Many blessing for you and don't forget to tell your son how much the Lord loves him!

Exodus 3: 14: *And God said unto Moses, **I AM THAT I AM:** and he said, Thus shalt thou say unto the children of Israel, **I AM** hath sent me unto you.*

Angels All Around Us

Ethan had been telling me for a while that occasionally he was seeing angels. One time I was sitting in my kitchen and we have a pass through window next to our dining room. As I sat at my computer working in the kitchen one night, I looked over into our dining room and I saw a translucent light figure of a person walking from the North to the South of our dining room. I knew three things about what I saw. It was clearly a figure of a person, the figure was moving and it was moving from the North end of the room toward the South end of the room. There was no question about what I saw. Ethan however, was reporting these sightings more frequently.

It was a cold, cold night and nine below zero. Ethan and I were driving together back from my Mom's place to home on a dark country road. We were having a conversation about Jesus. Ethan suddenly excitedly spoke up and told me there was someone in the car with us. I asked, "Who and where?" Ethan asked me if I saw him and I said, "No, where is he?" not knowing what he was talking about. Ethan then said there was an angel in the back seat of our car and the angel had touched him twice. Ethan felt a tingling feeling, which tickled him and made him laugh, and he said the angel was happy too. He said he saw the form of a person in the back seat. It was amazing the way Ethan was in such a good mood and sharing the moment seemingly with this other Holy being in our car.

I sent a few of my Christian friends an email about this wonderful occurrence. I also sent the story to my friend in Belgium. My Belgium friend wrote back in response to my description of our unusual experience. Therefore, I am including this amazing response to bless you. "Mrs. Anonymous" writes:

WOW! I didn't know what to think, so I asked the Lord and He started to speak to me immediately. He started to speak to me, and then He addresses Himself to Ethan, then to you, then to Ethan again. However, I have the impression this is a letter for all of us. The Lord is very excited! He keeps on telling me He will use me more and more for this, to encourage people, but this letter is so intense, even for me, and believe me, I am used to hearing Him speak, but this feels so intense. I have not experienced that many times. I am a bit shaking ... Here are the words of the Lord:

"Write it down, my daughter, I shall explain you the vision. Don't be afraid or concerned. This is My Voice. I tell you my daughter, this was my angel. This was one of the many angels who protect the child. This child has many angels around him. The more you pray, the more angels he will have at his disposal. He is my beloved child and I love his heart. He will be raptured so sure! I love your heart too my lovely daughter (He is talking to you now Susan). You will be raptured together. Do not be afraid my son (Ethan), I am always with you and your heart is very pleasing to Me. Stay close to Me and nothing or nobody shall harm

you. I am your Father and you are My son. I tell you, soon we will sit together at the wedding table of the Lamb and your joy shall be overflowing. I have so many surprises for my children. I am excited to take you all home. But pray for those who will be left behind. Pray my child, because this shall be their strength. This was My angel."

Praise the Lord for His love and care for His loved ones. How can we do anything but to love Him and praise Him? Thank you Jesus for being my Best Friend.

The New Jerusalem

Habakkuk 2:1: *I will stand at my watch and station myself on the ramparts; **I will look to SEE what he will SAY to me**, and what answer I am to give to this complaint.*

Sometime during the fall of 2007, I woke up around 3:00 a.m. in a *pitch-black* room with *no light* and with *my eyes closed,* I saw—all in red light only—a perfect, square that looked just like a building to me. I instantly thought of the dimensions of the New Jerusalem in the Bible and that is what came to mind at that moment. This image I saw lasted for about one minute and then it dissipated like water colors flowing off into opposite directions. Ever since, I cover my eyes and go in a perfectly dark room and I cannot make myself see something like this if I want to, no matter what I do. Several other people have since told me that I actually had a vision.

This is what the Bible says about the "square" dimensions of the New Jerusalem:

Revelation 21:15-21: *And he that talked with me had a golden reed to measure the city, and the gates thereof, and the wall thereof. **And the city lieth foursquare, and the length is as large as the breadth: and he measured the city with the reed, twelve thousand furlongs. The length and the breadth and the height of it are equal. And he measured the wall thereof, an hundred and forty and four cubits,** according to the measure of a man, that is, of the angel. And the building of the wall of it was of jasper: and the city was pure gold, like unto clear glass. And the foundations of the wall of the city were garnished with all manner of precious stones. The first foundation was jasper; the second, sapphire; the third, a chalcedony; the fourth, an emerald; The fifth, sardonyx; the sixth, sardius; the seventh, chrysolyte; the eighth, beryl; the ninth, a topaz; the tenth, a chrysoprasus; the eleventh, a jacinth; the twelfth, an amethyst. And the twelve gates were twelve pearls: every several gate was of one pearl: and the street of the city was pure gold, as it were transparent glass.*

The New Jerusalem is the home of the Bride—the Church, to share with the Father, Son, and Holy Spirit.

Over a year later one morning, when I first woke up the same thing happened as before. With my eyes completely shut, I saw a bright red light from the center of my field of vision. It was a circular shaped red light. Out from the center of the large red light, I saw an object emerge and it was a bright, bright white light object. At first, the emerging white light looked like a dove. Then the light very clearly became a round **wheel spinning**. There was a center point and a round outline and it was like a **wheel spinning** very fast. The **wheel** slowed down and I could see that it slowed to a stop and then everything just disappeared. The red light and everything became dark just like it is when you put your hands over your eyes normally.

I first thought in the vision I was seeing a propeller or a clock—but the Lord revealed that I was in fact seeing a wheel as you will see.

I had written about this vision to "Mrs. Anonymous" my friend in Belgium. She wrote me back:

Thank you very much for sharing your vision! As I am typing this, the Lord wants me to explain to you the visions:

The first one: *"The red light represents My blood, My precious blood that purifies everything. **My new city will be pure and clean. Nothing impure will enter it.**"*

The vision of this morning: *"The white light represents Myself. The **fast turning wheel** tells how I long to take My bride to Me. Once the **wheel** stops, I shall come, unexpected for those who don't expect me...splendor for the ones who do expect Me. I am coming soon and the **wheel** is losing its power. This is the revelation of your vision."*

I had no idea the Lord was going to reveal the meaning of these visions Susan. I just wanted to answer you and see what would happen. The Lord was very quick in saying He wanted to explain this. I said, Lord, You always explain dreams, but no visions (as I never had a vision), but He said even quicker: *"Then this is your first one!"* Then, He said that His Spirit was upon me.

This vision is also interesting perhaps from the standpoint that *"wheels"* are mentioned by both Ezekiel and Daniel as significant to visions they had of God's throne room.

Daniel 7:9: *I beheld till the thrones were cast down, and the Ancient of days did sit, whose garment was white as snow, and the hair of his head like the pure wool: his throne was like the fiery flame, and his **wheels** as burning fire.*

Ezekiel 10:1-22: *Then I looked, and, behold, in the firmament that was above the head of the cherubims there appeared over them as it were a sapphire stone, as the appearance of the likeness of a throne. And he spake unto the man clothed with linen, and said, Go in between the **wheels**, even under the cherub, and fill thine hand with coals of fire from between the cherubims, and scatter them over the city. And he went in in my sight. Now the cherubims stood on the right side of the house, when the man went in; and the cloud filled the inner court. Then the glory of the LORD went up from the cherub, and stood over the threshold of the house; and the house was filled with the cloud, and the court was full of the brightness of the LORD's glory. And the sound of the cherubims' wings was heard even to the outer court, as the voice of the Almighty God when he speaketh. And it came to pass, that when he had commanded the man clothed with linen, saying, Take fire from between the **wheels**, from between the cherubims; then he went in, and stood beside the **wheels**. And one cherub stretched forth his hand from between the cherubims unto the fire that was between the cherubims, and took thereof, and put it into the hands of him that was clothed with linen: who took it, and went out. And there appeared in the cherubims the form of a man's hand under their wings. And when I looked, behold the four **wheels** by the cherubims, one **wheel** by one cherub, and another **wheel** by another cherub: and the appearance of the **wheels** was as the color of a beryl stone. And as for their appearances, they four had one likeness, as if a **wheel** had been in the midst of a **wheel**. When they went, they went upon their four sides; they turned not as they went, but to the place whither the head looked they followed it; they turned not as they went. And their whole body, and their backs, and their hands, and their wings, and the **wheels**, were full of eyes round about, even the **wheels** that they four had. As for the **wheels**, it was cried unto them in my hearing, O **wheel**. And every one had four faces: the first face was the face of a cherub, and the second face was the face of a man, and the third the face of a lion, and the fourth the face of an eagle. And the cherubims were lifted up. This is the living creature that I saw by the river of Chebar. And when the cherubims went, the **wheels** went by them: and when the cherubims lifted up their wings to mount up from the earth, the same **wheels** also turned not from beside them When they stood, these stood; and when they were lifted up, these lifted up themselves also: for the spirit of the living creature was in them. Then the glory of the LORD departed from off the threshold of the house, and stood over the cherubims. And the cherubims lifted up their wings, and mounted up from the earth in my sight: when they went out, the **wheels** also were beside them, and every one stood at the door of the east gate of the LORD's house; and the glory of the God of Israel was over them above. This is the living creature that I saw under the God of Israel by the river of Chebar; and I knew that they were the cherubims. Every one had four faces apiece, and every one four wings; and the likeness of the hands of a man was under their wings. And the likeness of their faces was the same faces which I saw by the river of Chebar, their appearances and themselves: they went every one straight forward.*

Chapter Twenty-two—What I Have Learned...

What I Have Learned...

1. Isaiah 5:13: *Therefore my people are gone into captivity, because they have no knowledge: and their honorable men are famished, and their multitude dried up with thirst.*

You know I never used to have time for God, oh, maybe on Sunday morning or occasional Bible reading or prayer. However, when I started to seek God through more than prayer or church, but through reading about Him—I started to be amazed at how much I really did not know about God, Jesus, and the Holy Spirit. I began with reading the New Testament and then lots of books specifically written about God. There is so much in the Bible to discover about who God is and who we are, who we are to God, and what all this means. Had I not spent the time and given my time to these things that I would have probably used for other things, I would have missed so many valuable life-changing details found in the Bible that have meant so much to me. We could spend our whole life learning about God and only scratch the surface. Do not let this overwhelm you, because I have found that if you sincerely put forth the effort and interest, then the Holy Spirit will guide you in the direction He wants you to go in learning about God.

When you go in any library or Christian bookstore, you will find a ton of books written about how to improve your life, finances, family life, and how to fix life stressors. So many books are about a focus on us as individuals and working out our problems. Nevertheless, I discovered that when I read books purely about God, as far as who He is and what He is all about, I found that I learned so much about myself and who I am to God. Our identity is tied to who God is and learning about God leads to discovering who we are and what is the meaning of our life. Get to know God and you will find out indirectly who you are and why you even exist at all. The timeless classic book *"Imitation of Christ"* that was written by Thomas 'a Kempis around 1420 in the Netherlands, recorded these words about seeking God:

By seeking myself, I lost myself; by seeking you alone, and by loving you with a pure love, I found both myself and you. And through this love I have more profoundly returned to my nothingness, for you, O sweet Lord, you treat me far better than I deserve, beyond all that I dare to hope or to ask for.

www.ccel.org/ccel/kempis/imitation.toc.html

Another reason to read books written about God, in addition to the Bible, is to be enlightened about the meaning of the scripture that you may not understand. God gives different people understanding and revelations about His Word that others may not always see. That is why it can be very beneficial to read a variety of books about God written by godly writers. Sometimes I can reread a section of the Bible and something I have read over before that did not make sense, may come to life after the third time I read it. This is because the Holy Spirit allows you to see truth in the Bible that you may not have received before. Many times though, I have read a book written by someone with great God-given insight and the meaning of a Bible verse comes to life. (Be cautious however to read books written by people who acknowledge the Trinity of Father, Son, and Holy Spirit and that Jesus is the only way to salvation.)

The most efficient way to receive understanding of the Word of God is by praying to the Lord for guidance in understanding the Bible. Ask God to lead you in greater understanding of Him and His Word. This is surely in the will of God and will be a prayer God will answer.

One morning I had to fire up my laptop to send out an urgent email to someone and I thought I would just go ahead and work since the laptop was already on. I realized I had skipped right over my daily Bible reading and so I shrugged it off and decided to keep on working anyway.

At the moment, I thought about skipping my daily Bible reading and went back to work—the most amazing thing happened—my computer just shut off. Then I thought to myself, "I guess God is trying to tell me something," so instead of trying to turn on the computer again, I decided to read my Bible. Next I opened the Bible and I looked down at the first verse my eyes fell on and it was **Proverbs 12:1:** *Whoso loveth instruction loveth knowledge: but he that hateth reproof is brutish.*

2. Mark 12:30: *And thou shalt love the Lord thy God with all thy heart, and with all thy soul, and with all thy mind, and with all thy strength: this is the first commandment.*

This verse makes it clear to love God before anything or anyone else, yet there are still many Christians who question what this actually means to them. Some believe that Christians should blend with the world around them and fit in. However, the world does not accept God or know God so they do not actually adhere to this most important commandment. So why then do Christians believe that as Christians they should feel good about appearing like the world when God calls us to love Him with all of our heart, soul, mind, and strength? What does this look like? Does it look like a life devoted to the pursuit of money, position, entertainment, possessions or does it look like a life surrendered to Christ? If there were a line and the world was on one end and Jesus is on the opposite end—what point would your life fall on that line?

3. Romans 12:2: *And be not conformed to this world: but be ye transformed by the renewing of your mind, that ye may prove what is that good, and acceptable, and perfect, will of God.*

Many people can go to a church or an outreach event and answer an alter call to make Christ their Savior and they make that commitment. They can find a church to attend and go every Sunday morning. They can declare their commitment to Christ in front of others with water baptism. All of these are good *and necessary.* To stop here is wrong however. So many do not move forward at this point and make Jesus the undisputed *"Lord"* of their lives.

Jesus paid an enormous price to save you on the day He was whipped, humiliated, scourged, spit on, denied, abandoned, beaten, crucified, speared, maimed, and disfigured beyond recognition. He asks nothing less of us than that we give Him our life. And, what an exchange—we give Him our empty life of pursuing things that will lead to temporary satisfaction and eternal loss, traded for His abundant eternal river of life. Until we lay down our lives and give them to Him freely, our commitment to Christ is incomplete and when we run our lives apart from Jesus—we do not truly belong to Him.

Tell Christ how sincerely sorry you are for past sins and give Him your life. You agreed that Jesus died for your salvation, now lay your life at His feet. Please find a private place to be with God and get on your knees and pray for the Holy Spirit to fill you. Then you will be able to experience what the Bible describes as the filling of the Holy Spirit. Without being filled by the Holy Spirit, we are unable to experience the renewing of the mind Paul describes in the Bible. The renewing of the mind brought about by the Holy Spirit in your life leads you to greater understanding of being separate from the world, the importance of holiness, and seeking God in all things. Apart from this Holy Spirit baptism, your attempt to pursue holiness through the flesh and in your own effort will be impossible. You must be willing to surrender your complete life to Christ—not even holding back a portion of your life will be sufficient.

Titus 3:5: *Not by works of righteousness which we have done, but according to his mercy he saved us, by the washing of regeneration, and renewing of the Holy Ghost;*

4. Deuteronomy 4:29: *But if from thence thou shalt seek the LORD thy God, thou shalt find him, if thou seek him with all thy heart and with all thy soul.*

Seek the Lord your God with all your heart and all your soul sincerely and you will find Him. Just imagine—people will spend all eternity *with* God or *apart from* God. If you plan to spend eternity in Heaven, then you should want to begin seeking God *now* and spending time with Him because He will be the focus of your eternity in Heaven and spending time with God in His world as His own child. Do not wait too long to establish a relationship with the Lord in this life. Jesus warns that there will be people He tells in the next life, "I never knew you." How sad to think of and this is motivation to *seek God while He can be still be found.*

Imagine you spend your whole life ignoring God. Then at death, you expect to go to Heaven and not hell. Heaven is a life spent with and focused on God. You have not even bothered to call your Father on the phone and yet you expect to spend the next life in Heaven with Him 100 percent? Common sense says do not be shocked to learn that if you deny God your entire life and never receive Him as your Savior and Lord, then why would He think suddenly you want to spend all eternity with Him? Realize this truth now and *seek God while He can still be found.*

5. Matthew 5:6: *Blessed are they which do hunger and thirst after righteousness: for they shall be filled.*

This is one of my favorite Bible verses because it is so true. Apart from God, we are completely empty of holiness and righteousness. There is nothing within us on our own enabling us to be holy. Jesus urges us, "Be holy because I am holy." Therefore, we must sincerely ask God to be filled with holiness. God will begin to fill you and help you to understand about holiness versus sinful living apart from God and His holiness when you ask Him with a sincere heart. However, do not think you can seek holiness first to connect with God. That is impossible and the sooner you realize this, the quicker you will find your true place with God and the universe.

In fact, it is not enough for the individual to repent for sins and accept Christ as his savior even though this is required for justification of all our many sins to a holy God. The individual should also make a public declaration of receiving Christ as savior by means of a water baptism as well. Then he needs to make Christ more than just his Savior but also the Lord of his life. The new Christian needs to ask Christ to fill his life with the Holy Spirit. This necessary step after completed will enable the new Christian to be more fully able to read and understand the Bible, become a more dynamic witness of Christ, and to more readily comprehend and come to God's required righteousness. It is only through the infilling of God's Holy Spirit that anyone can really ever begin to conquer sin in their lives.

6. John 15:18: *If the world hates you, ye know that it hated me before it hated you.*

Christians, whether young or old, will experience persecution and sometimes from close friends and family members. Jesus guarantees this will happen. Jesus said they hate me and they will hate you too. The more boldly you speak out about Christ, the more likely you will be persecuted. Jesus says that He has overcome the world and He is with you always, no matter what you face. The world cannot accept God, but He promises blessings for those who are persecuted for His name's sake.

Persecution is rampant now. Persecution can be found among teens, office workers, family members, teachers, students, and others. Christ does not ask anyone to do anything that He has not experienced and He provides grace to endure whatever He places on you to experience. During some especially challenging periods of persecution, I received a very strong impression from God to focus all my energies on loving Him and He would take care of the rest.

7. Matthew 6:21: *For where your treasure is, there will your heart be also.*

If you put Christ at the center of your life as your one true treasure—you will never experience the disappointment you will with other things you put at the center of your life. Everything else in this life is temporal and ultimately will fail and let you down.

Job 22:21-26: *Acquaint now thyself with him, and be at peace: thereby good shall come unto thee. Receive, I pray thee, the law from his mouth, and lay up his words in thine heart. If thou return to the Almighty, thou* *shalt be built up, thou shalt put away iniquity far from thy tabernacles. Then shalt thou lay up gold as dust, and the gold of Ophir as the stones of the brooks. Yea, the Almighty shall be thy defence, and thou shalt have plenty of silver. For then shalt thou have thy delight in the Almighty, and shalt lift up thy face unto God.*

Psalms 16:5: *The LORD is the portion of mine inheritance and of my cup: thou maintainest my lot.*

Psalms 16:11: *Thou wilt shew me the path of life: in thy presence is fullness of joy; at thy right hand there are pleasures for evermore.*

8. John 15:15: *Henceforth I call you not servants; for the servant knoweth not what his lord doeth: but I have called you friends; for all things that I have heard of my Father I have made known unto you.*

I have decided that I do not want to wait until it is too late to have a serious relationship with Christ. It is too late to think about this when you are dying. I don't want to face Jesus someday and feel as if He is a complete stranger to me. God created us for companionship. How could we live a lifetime and give no credence to this thought? I want to be able to meet Jesus with great anticipation, as if I am meeting my best friend for the first time face-to-face. I want that moment to be the best moment of my existence.

Now is the best time to think about starting your relationship with Christ. Allow Him to come into your life as your Lord and Savior. Start your relationship with Jesus now, and you will come to understand more clearly, why it is you were created and why you even exist. You were created for relationship with God.

9. Luke 5:16: *And he withdrew himself into the wilderness, and prayed.*

Prayer to me is not a time to recite the same prayer to God over and over. God is our loving Father and deserves so much more of our time and consideration than to merely repeat the same dry words every time we decide to pray. Prayers should be sincere, caring, and addressed to God who is a real friend and our Father. God is not a far off, cold, unavailable being, but more so an omnipotent, omniscient, and sovereign friend who knows us better than we know ourselves. He deserves so much more than sterile, unfeeling prayers, and just being scheduled into the tiny time slots in our busy lives. He gives us everything—He created us, His Son Jesus died a hideous death to save us, and He will be our complete focus for eternity. So today is the time to start our eternal relationship with Him.

10. Matthew 7:14: *Because straight is the gate, and narrow is the way, which leadeth unto life, and few there be that find it.*

I pray sincerely that if the road to Heaven is narrow and the road to hell is broad, then please Lord get me to that narrow road. I believe the Lord will hear you if you sincerely pray this prayer. Jesus is the narrow road and if you ask to know Him better, He will honor your request.

11. Jeremiah 29:11: *For I know the thoughts that I think toward you, saith the LORD, thoughts of peace, and not of evil, to give you an expected end.*

When you surrender your life to the Lord, why not pray that He would take it and apply His perfect plan to it? Really if God made you, He must also have a perfect plan to apply to that life. Ask Him to apply *His* perfect plan to your life.

12. Hebrews 13:8: *Jesus Christ the same yesterday, and today, and forever.*

God is
"supernatural"

God created the world
"supernaturally"

God sustains the world
"supernaturally"

Jesus came into the world
"supernaturally"

Jesus performs miracles
"supernaturally"

God's Holy Spirit Lives within us
"supernaturally"

So if Christians can accept that "Jesus is the same yesterday, today, and forever" (because the Bible says it is so) and that "God does not change like shifting shadows," why then do Christians today squirm so when you speak of the things Jesus spoke of: angels, demons, satan, miraculous healing, hearing the audible voice of God, visions, signs and wonders, speaking in other languages, and receiving prophetic words?

In Jeremiah, the Bible speaks of a king who "edited" the Word of God as given to the Prophet Jeremiah by cutting and burning the parts he did not like. Christians today behave like this king and choose to disregard things in the Bible as if they do not apply in today's world.

Jeremiah 36:20-32: *And they went in to the king into the court, but they laid up the roll in the chamber of Elishama the scribe, and told all the words in the ears of the king. So the king sent Jehudi to fetch the roll: and he took it out of Elishama the scribe's chamber. And Jehudi read it in the ears of the king, and in the ears of all the princes which stood beside the king. Now the king sat in the winterhouse in the ninth month: and there was a fire on the hearth burning before him. And it came to pass, that when Jehudi had read three or four leaves, he cut it with the penknife, and cast it into the fire that was on the hearth, until all the roll was consumed in the fire that was on the hearth. Yet they were not afraid, nor rent their garments, neither the king, nor any of his servants that heard all these words. Nevertheless Elnathan and Delaiah and Gemariah had made intercession to the king that he would not burn the roll: but he would not hear them. But the king commanded Jerahmeel the son of Hammelech, and Seraiah the son of Azriel, and Shelemiah the son of Abdeel, to take Baruch the scribe and Jeremiah the prophet: but the LORD hid them. Then the word of the LORD came to Jeremiah, after that the king had burned the roll, and the words which Baruch wrote at the mouth of Jeremiah, saying, Take thee again another roll, and write in it all the former words that were in the first roll, which Jehoiakim the king of Judah hath burned. And thou shalt say to Jehoiakim king of Judah, Thus saith the LORD; Thou hast burned this roll, saying, Why hast thou written therein, saying, The king of Babylon shall certainly come and destroy this land, and shall cause to cease from thence man and beast? Therefore thus saith the LORD of Jehoiakim king of Judah; He shall have none to sit upon the throne of David: and his dead body shall be cast out in the day to the heat, and in the night to the frost. And I will punish him and his seed and his servants for their iniquity; and I will bring upon them, and upon the inhabitants of Jerusalem, and upon the men of Judah, all the evil that I have pronounced against them; but they hearkened not. Then took Jeremiah another roll, and gave it to Baruch the scribe, the son of Neriah; who wrote therein from the mouth of Jeremiah all the words of the book which Jehoiakim king of Judah had burned in the fire: and there were added besides unto them many like words.*

I can show you how God is supernatural by simply handing you an orange. Take an orange seed and plant it in the ground and from it a tree grows. Then it blossoms with beautiful flowers and produces a lovely fragrance. Then round, brightly colored fruit appears covered in a secure leather-like casing. Tear through the tough yet easily opened casing and find a flavorful food already divided into sections. But is it merely a food or is it also a wonderful tasting drink? Look inside the orange and find more seeds to grow more oranges. Why it is ingenious and also *miraculous* in its design. The orange is a divine gift from a supernatural God.

2 Peter 3:3: *Knowing this first, that there shall come in the last days scoffers, walking after their own lusts,*

Jude 1:18: *How that they told you there should be mockers in the last time, who should walk after their own ungodly lusts.*

13. Isaiah 26:3: *Thou wilt keep him in perfect peace, whose mind is stayed on thee: because he trusteth in thee.*

Do not tell someone that they are spending too much time focusing on God. At what point does someone decide that they have spent too much time with the Lord? How many hours a week or a day is too much? The answer is it is impossible to spend too much time with the Lord.

1 Thessalonians 5:17 says: *Pray without ceasing.* And Jesus prayed frequently when He was on earth. How much more do we need to pray and lean into God ourselves if even Jesus did?

Colossians 3:1-4: *If ye then be risen with Christ, seek those things which are above, where Christ sitteth on the right hand of God. Set your affection on things above, not on things on the earth. For ye are dead, and your life is hid with Christ in God. When Christ, who is our life, shall appear, then shall ye also appear with him in glory.*

I have a dear friend who suggested to me one time that some people "are too Heavenly-minded to be any Earthly good." I thought about this and I wondered if it is possible for Christians to be too Heavenly-minded to be any Earthly good? Incredibly, I did not need to ponder too long, because the next day I came across the editor's comment in my *"New Living Translation New Believer's Bible"* in Isaiah which addressed this very issue. The commentary says that the exact opposite is true.

Matthew 6:19-21: *Lay not up for yourselves treasures upon earth, where moth and rust doth corrupt, and where thieves break through and steal: But lay up for yourselves treasures in heaven, where neither moth nor rust doth corrupt, and where thieves do not break through nor steal: For where your treasure is, there will your heart be also.*

14. Matthew 6:11: *Give us this day our daily bread.*

People think that what has been written in the Bible in the past does not have messages that hold true for our lives today. One such message repeated in the Bible is the message about living in the moment today and not beating yourself up over the past and not trying to plan and live in the future. The Bible says that Christ explains that it is arrogant and evil to say you are going somewhere in the future to make a profit when only God really knows what the next hour holds.

One of the reasons this is so wrong to God is that we have a tendency to want to idolize our careers, our 401Ks, our houses, our retirement plans, our plans for the future, and our possessions over our value for God. We put stock in things dangerously as our security when only God is truly our security. The danger of this is we ourselves are not God and we cannot know the future. When we try to plan and look to our own plans, then things fall apart because the economy fails us, our company fails us, or our position is eliminated, and that is when we meet failure head on. We have to come to the end of ourselves and then we finally are willing to humble ourselves before God, turn in our (future planning) weapons, and surrender to Him.

Once we drop our own plans and give them over to Christ and we say to Him that we want His plans for our life and not ours—then Jesus can put His plans for our life into action. Then the most amazing thing can happen. We step aside from our arrogance and our view that we know best and then we can stand back and let God move into action on our behalf. Then we can see God shape our lives into the plans He has for us which is always going to be much bigger and better than what we can plan for ourselves, if only we can let go and let God take over.

Another problem with not submitting our need to depend on ourselves and not God's plans for us is that we do not know the future. In addition, the dilemma of not knowing the future can cause us to worry needlessly and to become obsessed about preparing for a future we cannot predict. This creates greed, workaholics, hording money and possessions, and unwarranted worry. This emphasis we place in our own plans and not God's plans, causes us to spend time on things we think will bring us security instead of focusing on spending time with God. Sadly, we miss the prime directive for our very existence and that is to love God with all our heart, with all our soul, and with all our strength. How can we do this when we are trapped in generating security for ourselves for a future we know nothing about?

What if God revealed to you that you would not live for more than a year, how differently would you live your life? If you knew that you only had one year to live—would you spend it building up your personal savings account or would you spend more time getting to know God?

Here are some verses that speak on the subject of living for today and not worrying about tomorrow:

Matthew 6:34: *Take therefore no thought for the morrow: for the morrow shall take thought for the things of itself. Sufficient unto the day is the evil thereof.*

Luke 12:22-26: *And he said unto his disciples, Therefore I say unto you, Take no thought for your life, what ye shall eat; neither for the body, what ye shall put on. The life is more than meat, and the body is more than raiment. Consider the ravens: for they neither sow nor reap; which neither have storehouse nor barn; and God feedeth them: how much more are ye better than the fowls? And which of you with taking thought can add to his stature one cubit? If ye then be not able to do that thing which is least, why take ye thought for the rest?*

Luke 12:16-21: *And he spake a parable unto them, saying, The ground of a certain rich man brought forth plentifully: And he thought within himself, saying, What shall I do, because I have no room where to bestow my fruits? And he said, This will I do: I will pull down my barns, and build greater; and there will I bestow all my fruits and my goods. And I will say to my soul, Soul, thou hast much goods laid up for many years; take thine ease, eat, drink, and be merry. But God said unto him, Thou fool, this night thy soul shall be required of thee: then whose shall those things be, which thou hast provided? So is he that layeth up treasure for himself, and is not rich toward God.*

15. 1 Peter 1:14-16: *As obedient children, not fashioning yourselves according to the former lusts in your ignorance: But as he which hath called you is holy, so be ye holy in all manner of conversation; Because it is written, Be ye holy; for I am holy.*

The same satanic evil force that incited terrorists to destroy the Twin Towers in New York and to cause Nazi Germany to commit racial cleansing, that same evil that cause us to be incensed at the outrageousness of these acts, is the same exact evil force inside us that causes us to lie or hurt others. We so easily hurt our family, friends, and co-workers in little ways and we do not even give it a second thought. Then we watch the news and see somebody taking a hostage or killing their own family and themselves and we shudder in horror thinking we cannot relate to this kind of incredible evil. Yet God's rule of order says all of our righteousness is as filthy rags.

To God a little sin is not okay any more than a lot of sin is wrong. If God did not call all sin wrong—no matter how small in our eyes—then where precisely does he draw the line? How much sin is okay and how much sin is overboard? That is how humans judge. Each person creates his or her own ratio factor of what amount of sin is acceptable and what is not.

One man may cheat on his wife and then watch the nightly news and think that what happened on 9/11 is shockingly wrong. That is what Hollywood does all the time. The heroes fighting so-called evil foes are cursing and sleeping with women they just met and we look on as if this is normal and acceptable. However, to God, all sin is evil including swearing and adultery. Yes, terrorism is blatantly evil, but so is the way I hurt someone's feelings when I am inconsiderate. The same evil force is at play in both situations and to God sin is sin.

God's mercy (receiving forgiveness we do not deserve) and grace (receiving a gift we do not deserve) is also outrageous. We need God's forgiveness and grace through the blood of Christ whether we hurt someone's feelings or whether we commit an act of terrorism. Amazingly, because all sin is the same to God, the precious and ever-available blood of Christ can equally forgive a white lie as well as someone else's shocking heinous crime. Thank God for the precious blood of Christ.

When we surrender our lives to Christ and invite the Holy Spirit to come into our lives, the Holy Spirit will come in and help us to fight the satanic evil that terrorizes and incites everyone to commit evil acts, big and small. Men cannot discern evil in their lives apart from God and they cannot see that even small things are outrageous and wrong to our just and holy pure God. I am thankful that God is the ultimate judge and not men in their distorted and confused human value system. I thank God that we can turn to Him for truth and direction for our lives and we have but to ask Him for it.

God is the perfect judge because He sees all, knows all, and even knows the inner hearts and motives of men so then He is able to render absolute undeniable true justice.

The evangelist Charles H. Spurgeon wrote in his book *"According to Promise"* this statement about God and sin:

Neither doth the Lord deal with men according to the measure of their moral ability. "Oh," says the seeker, "I think I might be saved if I could make myself better, or become more religious, or exercise greater faith; but I am without strength, I cannot believe; I cannot repent; I cannot do anything right!" Remember, then, that the Gracious God has not promised to bless you according to the measure of your ability to serve Him, but according to the riches of His grace as declared in His Word. If His gifts were bestowed according to your spiritual strength, you would get nothing; for you can do nothing without the Lord.

When I think of the sin of jealousy, I think how sad it must make God when people become envious of each other. Well obviously jealously leads to lots of sadness between people who are jealous of each other and the things they have. But really what I think must hurt God the most is when we envy others' possessions and positions in life because we are yet unable to find satisfaction in God and we are still longing after the things of the world. I think this must really grieve God. I hope we can get to a point where we can see all the wealth others have or their stations in life and it will not even faze us because we are so satiated with God.

Chapter Twenty-three—My Grandmother's Final Instruction

My Grandmother's Final Instruction:

This will be appreciated by anyone who wants a relationship with Christ. The following actually was my maternal Grandmother Mary Ann McKinniss' final instruction to her family written many years ago:

I'm persuaded that He is able to keep that which I've committed unto Him that day.

My advice to my children, grandchildren, and great grandchildren:

The first thing to do is to get acquainted with Christ your Savior and Lord. Just to know of Him and about Him won't do, you must put Him first in your life. Love Him more than anything else.

You must put Him above education, power, fame, and things of this world. They are so helpless and worthless without your Savior, so He must be first to make other things worthwhile.

He is the way to the pearly gates and the streets of gold. My plea, as your Mother, Grandmother, and Great Grandmother is to make Him your Master Companion and Guide. Keep hold of His nail-pierced hand.

To all my neighbors, dear friends, and people everywhere this is my same advice.

Really know Christ your Redeemer and King. A wonderful Savior is Jesus your Lord. He is coming soon, be ready! -*My Grandmother, Mary Ann McKinniss*

O, What Would I Do?

This Monday morning is what I call blue
If it wasn't for Jesus—O, what would I do?
I've sought Him for comfort, refuge, and rest
And I know He will guide me wherever is best,

I fled to my secret place of prayer
Feeling sure Jesus would meet me there,
And that His presence would dispel my blues
And help me His counsel to willingly choose.

In Christ, I find sweet comfort and peace
From blues in Him I find release,
He always helps me along life's way
If I seek His divine presence from day to day,

O Lord, help to live so close to thee
That my faith will not waver and blues will flee,
And, sweet contentment in Jesus I'll find
Singing all the way, Hallelujah, Jesus is mine,

How since my talk with Jesus I've had
Instead of blues, I feel so very glad,
In Him, I find a cheery friend so true
If it wasn't for Jesus, O, what would I do?
-Mary Ann McKinniss

Useful Resources:

"The Jesus Visions," by Christine Darg, the entire book is available online at
www.jesusvisions.org/index.html

"Message from God" by former Mrs. South Africa Retha McPherson and her son Aldo McPherson,
available at www.Rethamcpherson.com or Amazon

Self-Talk from the Scriptures™ CDs founded by Princess LaVear are available through Living Word
Enterprises, available at www.berenewed.com or Amazon

Living Balls Ministry in South Africa founded by former South African professional rugby player Manie
du Toit found at www.livingballs.com

"Devotional Commentary on the Song of Solomon" by Esher Shoshannah, the entire book is available
online at www.songofsolomondevotional.com

Bibles at Cost Bibles for ordering affordable Bibles in bulk at cost for outreach can be
found at www.biblesatcost.com

Seek God Ministries for "finding God" resources are available at www.seekgod.org

"Heaven Researched" research notes available per request by emailing: **lovethewhirlwind@sbcglobal.net**

If you would also like to be **"In Love with the Whirlwind"** *and for God to take your heart by storm*, we
would love to hear from you. If you would like the author to speak at your next group event or to contact
the author, Susan Davis, write to **lovethewhirlwind@sbcglobal.net**

Contact *"In Love with the Whirlwind"* designer at **BluePawCreations@yahoo.com**